Mobile Marketing

Second Edition

Mobile Marketing

How mobile technology is
revolutionizing marketing,
communications and advertising

Daniel Rowles

KoganPage

Publisher's note

Every possible effort has been made to ensure that the information contained in this book is accurate at the time of going to press, and the publisher and author cannot accept responsibility for any errors or omissions, however caused. No responsibility for loss or damage occasioned to any person acting, or refraining from action, as a result of the material in this publication can be accepted by the editor, the publisher or the author.

First published in Great Britain and the United States in 2014 by Kogan Page Limited
Second edition published in 2017

2nd Floor, 45 Gee Street	c/o Martin P Hill Consulting	4737/23 Ansari Road
London EC1V 3RS	122 W 27th St, 10th Floor	Daryaganj
United Kingdom	New York NY 10001	New Delhi 110002
www.koganpage.com	USA	India

© Daniel Rowles, 2014, 2017

ISBN   978 0 7494 7979 4
E-ISBN 978 0 7494 7980 0

British Library Cataloguing-in-Publication Data

A CIP record for this book is available from the British Library.

Library of Congress Cataloging-in-Publication Data

CIP data is available.

Library of Congress Control Number: 2016043263

Typeset by Graphicraft Limited, Hong Kong
Print production managed by Jellyfish
Printed and bound by CPI Group (UK) Ltd, Croydon, CR0 4YY

CONTENTS

LIST OF FIGURES

FOREWORD

It's clear that mobile devices are having a profound impact not only on how we communicate on a daily basis, but also on how we interact and engage with individuals and organizations of all types.

At the Chartered Institute of Marketing (CIM) we see time and time again that practitioners, and those studying business of any type (whether they consider themselves marketers or not), need a better understanding of the digital landscape. We also see that landscape changing incredibly quickly and that mobile is playing a major part in this.

In this fast-changing environment, knowledge of both the strategic impact and the tactical issues around mobile marketing will become increasingly important, particularly as this naturally overlaps into areas such as social media.

Daniel has worked extensively with CIM, helping our members and customers to navigate their way through this exciting and fast-moving environment. He is a respected authority on all things digital and as such is the ideal guide for your mobile marketing journey.

Chris Daly, Chief Executive, CIM

ACKNOWLEDGEMENTS

There are many people who have encouraged and assisted me in writing this book and I have named a few of them here.

Firstly, to the small and perfectly formed Target Internet team. Very special thanks to Susana, our incredible commercial director, without whom we wouldn't have the successful business we have today (she is also a dab hand at back-office admin!). Thanks to Ciaran for motivating and cajoling me to keep things on track generally, and for letting me steal his ideas (particularly on the future of mobile in the transport industry. I'm not so grateful for his obsession with QR codes!). Thank you to Marie for her tireless efforts in making my ramblings into professional-looking content every month. Many thanks to Hemangi for her incredible hard work and expertise in building our technical assets. Thank you to Pete, our newest team member, for making me realize I need to up my game in writing and for constantly giving us a fresh and engaging tone.

Another huge thank you to the very inspirational and talented Jonathan Macdonald for making the introduction that led to this book (and its second edition!). The free wine is on me next time we spend 12 hours in an airport lounge.

And finally, a massive thank you to all of you who read this book, visit Target Internet, listen to the Digital Marketing podcast, follow me on Twitter and very kindly give me an audience with whom to engage and share my ideas.

This book is dedicated to my ever patient, beautiful and straight-talking wife Susana, without whom it would still be on a to-do list somewhere.

This is also a great opportunity to get my kids' names in print, so they can show all their friends and I can score many, many 'awesome dad' points. I love you both dearly, Teresa and Charlie.

Introduction

Mobile is not a channel like social media, outdoor advertising or search; it is something that impacts all of the other marketing channels, both online and offline. It is a fundamental shift in human behaviour that we need to understand, and we need to adjust how we operate accordingly. We can't separate 'mobile marketing' from other marketing activity, and therefore the very term itself can be misleading. Mobile Marketing is dead!

This book aims to be a practical guide to understanding and using mobile marketing for organizations of different types and sizes around the globe. However, in order to do this, we need to start by defining what we really mean by mobile marketing.

Looking in the wrong direction

The most common mistake made in mobile marketing is to focus on the device. When we focus on the smartphone or tablet that someone is using we instantly start to look in the wrong direction. I'll explain why.

How big does a phone need to get before it becomes a tablet? What about if my laptop has a touchscreen? Does it then become a tablet? What if my tablet has a keyboard? Is it still a mobile device? The reality is that the merging and extremely fast evolution of mobile devices is already out of date by the time we have adjusted to it.

What we need is a strategy and an implementation plan that allow us to make maximum use of the technology available without getting bogged down with the devices we are planning for (although we will address device planning later in this book).

Focus on the user journey

Mobile marketing is actually all about understanding the user journey. Understanding what individuals (even when acting as part of larger organizations) want to achieve. This could be anything from educating themselves to booking a cinema ticket, but whatever the objective, we need to understand how the technologies that make up mobile marketing can be used to help achieve the goals of an individual.

The human element

Our mobile devices are by nature very personal to us. We carry them with us, use them when we are moving from place to place and they help make our lives easier (or at least should do!) If I try and broadcast generic marketing messages through your mobile device they are even less likely to work than through other channels. Generally speaking, when you are on a mobile device you have less time, you are focused on a specific goal and you are 'in the moment'. And this is exactly why mobile marketing is so essential and requires us to think about marketing in a very different way.

Disruption

As you work through this book you'll learn about the practicalities of building apps, mobile websites and technologies like near field communication (NFC). All we are really doing, though, is arming ourselves with tools for a world where the shift in marketing has been profound.

We'll explore how media consumption has radically changed, how people are using multiple screens at once (think how often you watch TV without a smartphone to hand) and how the idea of a mobile device starts to become obsolete when you are wearing those devices (we'll explore this later too).

So what can we do in such a fast-changing and disruptive market? We focus on the basics.

Back to basics

I've worked with many of the world's largest and fastest-changing organizations over the last 18 years, advising them how they can best use digital technologies to achieve their business objectives. No matter what the topic, be it social media search optimization or e-mail marketing (both of which are part of mobile marketing), I always come back to basics. Set your objectives, understand your target audience, select the appropriate tools, channels and content and then deploy, test and learn. Mobile marketing is absolutely essential and mobile marketing is dead.

How to get the most out of this book

The book is split into three key parts.

Part One Mobile marketing in perspective

This part will give you an understanding of who the mobile consumer is, a core view of the technology involved and how it impacts you, and finally, how to set objectives for your mobile marketing.

Part Two Tactical toolkit

This part explores the core technologies, techniques and tools involved in mobile marketing. Here we explore things like mobile payments, mobile sites, apps and NFC. Jump straight to this section if you need some hands-on tips and techniques.

Part Three Checklists

This short and final section will help you set a mobile strategy and make sure you aren't missing anything. It comprises some practical checklists and a step-by-step planning tool for creating your mobile strategy.

You can also get all the latest on mobile marketing by visiting http://www.targetinternet.com/mobilemarketing.

PART ONE
Mobile marketing in perspective

Introduction 01

It's very easy to start thinking about mobile marketing from the perspective of the tactics we are planning to implement: that great idea for an app, a beautifully designed responsive website or a clever idea for using mobile payments. The reality, just with any digital marketing activity, is that it's generally a very good idea to take a step back and fully understand what we are trying to achieve and the environment we are working in.

Part One therefore is all about understanding the broader environment we are working in. It will help you understand who the mobile consumer is, get a core view of the technology involved and finally show you how to set objectives for your mobile marketing.

This core knowledge will help you inform your strategy before you start to embark on the tactical journey of implementing your mobile marketing campaigns (which is covered in detail in Part Two).

Although this section explores some of the latest statistics and developments in mobile marketing, we also acknowledge that this is a fast-paced environment with constant change. For that reason, we have pointed out numerous resources along the way, as well as compiling the best of these on our website.

This first part of the book is also here to stop you wasting time and money by highlighting some of the key risks of mobile marketing. It is very easy to be seduced by new technologies that offer fantastic creative opportunities. However, without the grounding of how this fits into an overall strategy and a clear measurement framework to tie things back to our objectives, there is huge potential to be very busy without being productive in any way.

I still see, on an almost daily basis, Facebook pages for the sake of Facebook pages and mobile apps for the sake of apps. This generally starts in one of two ways. Either somebody senior says, 'Why don't we have an app? Go make an app!' or somebody comes up with a half-baked idea that starts its life without any proper planning. The end results are generally disappointing and costly. This then gives the impression that mobile is costly, complicated and ineffective. In reality, any marketing done in this way is generally a disaster.

This section, however, is not about looking at the negative. It's all about embracing the huge and exciting potential that mobile marketing offers and doing so in a risk-mitigated way. This will help you make the most of your resources and should save you a lot of stress.

What Part One will help you do

- Make sure you have a clear view of the environment you are working in.
- Understand how mobile makes up part of the user journey.
- Set your objectives and understand the mobile technologies that might help you achieve these objectives.
- Highlight some of the key risks you will face along your mobile marketing journey.
- Understand how to cope with a fast-changing environment and see how our website can help you stay up to date and on top of the latest developments: http://www.targetinternet.com/mobilemarketing.

Understanding the user journey

02

We can now interact with businesses from pretty much anywhere we have some form of internet connection. On the bus, travelling by train or whilst walking along. This image of mobile marketing being all about mobility in its purest sense is often used, but defies the reality of how we are actually using mobile devices in the majority of cases. Most mobile usage is done at home, in the office or somewhere else stationary, and most of it is about 'me' time (Gevelber, 2016).

So if it's actually not about using your phone when moving, why is Hotels.com's 'Hotel Booked in Freefall' video (TheJTHolmes, 2011) so successful (attracting over 1 million views in YouTube at time of publishing) and often quoted as a great example, as it is in Google's excellent Mobile Playbook.

Well, first of all it's a fun and engaging concept that grabs your attention. Somebody trying to book a hotel room on a phone whilst jumping out of a plane is a fairly extreme idea! However, it achieves its objectives as a piece of marketing because it demonstrates and reinforces a key value pro-position. That is the idea that Hotels.com makes it quick and easy to book hotels.

This alignment with value proposition and what the consumer actually wants is essential, and although it sounds obvious, is more often than not completely missed in mobile marketing campaigns. The reason that this basic concept of alignment with consumer requirements is missed is that we (or the partners and agencies we work with) are blinded by the technology and creative options.

The consumer and business-to-business

Very often when we talk about 'mobile consumers' we immediately start to think about somebody buying a product in a shop or a website. However, I think we should look at the consumer in a broader context, and part of this will include anyone that is engaging with our mobile marketing in some way.

For this reason, when we talk about the mobile consumer, we will also be considering those making business-to-business (B2B) purchasing decisions. Clearly the requirements of somebody checking the reviews of a movie are very different to those of somebody checking information on the supplier they are about to meet, but they do hold the same principle in common. That is, that we need to understand what this consumer is trying to achieve and in what context.

In many cases mobile marketing is dismissed in the B2B environment as something that is more suited to business-to-consumer (B2C) marketing, but I would argue that the whole point of mobile is its personal nature and the need to understand the target audience's objectives and context.

Business users mix their personal and business time on mobile devices, and with social platforms like LinkedIn it is possible for this line to become even further blurred. For example, I may be relaxing and staying up to date with my social contacts and I may be looking at the LinkedIn app as part of this.

We clearly need to look at B2B and B2C marketing differently, but many of the same core principles apply. At the core of this is understanding our target users' needs and context, then using mobile marketing to service these needs and making sure they align with our business objectives.

Technology for the sake of technology

Just because we can build an app doesn't mean we should (in fact you really need to think about mobile sites before apps in the majority of cases, but more on that later). Using technology inappropriately without setting objectives or having a clear business case is nothing new.

From my experience, the majority of business Twitter and Facebook accounts are set up with little or no idea whatsoever of why they're being created. It happens because somebody senior has decided it's a good idea without understanding it, somebody junior did it without asking anyone, or someone in the business has seen that competitors are doing it so feel an opportunity is being missed. It doesn't mean it's necessarily the wrong channel or a bad idea, but anything done without objectives or a business case is generally doomed to failure.

This lack of strategy isn't isolated to mobile marketing. One of my favourite examples demonstrates how this applies to digital marketing generally. Dave Chaffey is a well-respected digital marketing author (as well as being an excellent lecturer, public speaker and someone whose opinion I respect). He runs a website called SmartInsights.com that provides digital marketing advice and stimulates conversation on the topic. As such he regularly asks his audience how many of them are carrying out any form of digital marketing and how many of them have a strategy behind this activity. Every time this questionnaire is run, the results come back the same. Nearly 70 per cent of those asked are carrying out digital marketing activities with no strategy. Although this is only a small sample survey, it does identify a key trend that I can back up from my many years of working with organizations to improve their digital marketing efforts.

Now, to be fair, this 70 per cent might be doing the right things, for the right reason, measuring effectively and achieving their business objectives. Although I'm pretty sure that's not the case for all of them. Even if it were, they probably wouldn't know it, as they have no strategy against which to measure their success.

User journey and context

Understanding the user journey is going to be essential to the success of our mobile marketing, so let's try and understand this in a bit more detail. We need to understand what our target audience might want to achieve, understand their path to doing this, see how mobile fits in, and then provide the right experiences and content to achieve these objectives.

Some of this will be the 'discovery phase' (also referred to as push, stimulus and in a dozen other ways!) where we are trying to build awareness, educate and stimulate some form of further action.

Some will be in the 'engagement phase'. These are activities that are driving engagement, experiences and moving toward the users' final objectives.

Table 2.1 Discovery and engagement phases in mobile marketing

Discovery Phase	Engagement Phase
Mobile e-mail	Mobile sites
Mobile display ads	Apps
Mobile paid search	Mobile-optimized social
Mobile organic search	Mobile payment and couponing
Offline stimulus (QR codes, etc)	Location-based interaction (NFC etc)
Push notifications	

The different techniques and technologies are shown in Table 2.1, and we'll explore them in more detail in Part Two of this book. However, we first need to identify how they fit together.

The line between discovery and engagement becomes increasingly blurred as we move into location-based interaction (engaging with a brand when in-store, for example), but these phases can start to lay a foundation for us when thinking about where mobile fits into the user journey. However, this is currently a fairly one-dimensional model that only really talks about mobile marketing techniques, whilst acknowledging that things like offline marketing may exist.

Mobile and multi-channel marketing

The reality of all marketing is that there generally isn't one thing that makes you buy a product or choose a supplier. Generally, there is a huge range of factors that make you prefer one brand over another, choose a supplier or buy a particular detergent. Marketing is all about understanding this process.

As marketers we can model, measure and use all sorts of tools to try and understand this buying process, and this is where digital marketing has its greatest strengths. We have access to more data and more capability to measure the user journey than ever before. However, the missing piece in this measurement puzzle has been the interaction between online and offline marketing. We'll still face some challenges with this, but quite often mobile can act as the bridge between offline and online.

Mobile marketing will generally be part of the user journey and many other channels may be involved, some digital and some not. The journey is very unlikely to be a linear one, and many channels and types of content may be revisited several times, in no particular order, and we may not have any visibility on many of the steps in the journey.

A multi-screen journey

As well as needing to consider a wide range of channels being involved in any user journey, we need to realize that there will also be a number of different 'screens' involved, and very often we will be using multiple screens at the same time. For example, at key TV viewing times, around 80 per cent us will be watching TV whilst using another device (Young, 2016).

To consider the full range of screens we need to take into account smart-phones, tablet devices, desktops/laptops, wearables (such as smart watches), TV and, with the advent of driverless cars and the increase in driver services such as Uber, in-car screens. This broadens our view of mobile to such an extent that the only way to address it effectively is to focus on the user journey.

The growth of in-vehicle screens

With the advent of widely adopted driving services such as Uber and Didi (the largest car-hailing app in China), we are increasingly using our mobile devices whilst travelling by road. However, this is only the tip of the iceberg in regard to in-vehicle screen viewing when we consider the imminent growth of driverless cars.

If you are on your 45-minute commute in a driverless car, your attention clearly won't be needed for driving. So what will you be doing with your time? You'll be looking at a screen, and I'm sure initially this will be on your own mobile devices. However, consider the fact that the entire car interior is currently geared toward the driver and driving position. As this becomes unnecessary, the entire car interior can be focused on entertainment and interaction. Why use your tiny mobile device screen, when the entire car interior could be dedicated to having interactive screens? It's early days at the time of writing for driverless cars, but already companies like Ford are patenting ideas for radical new car interiors focused on bringing more screens into the vehicle (McMahon, 2016).

User journey examples

Let's take a look at two real-world user journeys all the way through to purchase and consider how different channels are working together.

B2B example

I need a new hosting company for my business website. I'm responsible for the website's reliability and I have had some bad experiences previously, ending in my website being down and me being frustrated and embarrassed. This buying decision is primarily motivated by risk mitigation, but I also need to make sure that my website will be fast and any provider will give me the opportunity to expand and improve my web offering, so I need flexibility and performance. This is not a decision I will make without being well informed and the user journey is made up of multiple steps, including, but not limited to:

- doing numerous searches for suppliers;
- reading online reviews of these suppliers;
- signing up for newsletters from each of these suppliers;
- asking opinions from my social network on LinkedIn and Twitter of their experiences;
- completing several diagnostic tools to understand what kind of hosting I actually need;
- reading websites that talk about the technology behind hosting to educate myself about the technology;
- signing up for newsletters from the sites that helped me educate myself;
- talking to colleagues and trusted partners at unrelated events and meetings;
- getting recommendations for suppliers I had never heard of and making a note on my phone.

On first inspection, the only step in this journey that specifically used a mobile device was making a note of recommended suppliers. The reality, however, is that a great deal of this research was actually done when I was in a hotel, travelling by train or on a plane. I also use multiple devices, including a laptop, a tablet and a smartphone.

So let's map out what's important to note in this user journey. Firstly, that my decision is being based on risk mitigation and finding the right fit to my needs. I also need to educate myself on the topic (which is very common in B2B buying decisions).

We also need to note the practicalities of this journey. It was done almost entirely online, except where face-to-face word of mouth was involved. However, I only knew to search for several suppliers because I was already aware of them due to some other offline interaction at previous trade shows. Also, much of the time I was reading and educating myself I was actually offline as I had no internet access (on a plane or on a train with poor connectivity).

So what does this tell us about our mobile marketing planning? Well, our value proposition needs to align closely with the ideas of risk mitigation, trust and education. So a clear value proposition aligned to user needs at the heart of any strategy would be essential for any potential supplier.

The suppliers needed to provide more content than just telling me how great their solution was. I needed education to build trust. This is a classic example of the need for content marketing, which we'll discuss shortly.

I relied on my social network and online reviews heavily to influence my decision. An effective social media approach was also clearly going to be essential for any potential supplier, and how I experienced this on different devices would need to be considered.

As well as needing these different types of content I needed to be able to consume them in ways that suited me. And what suited me varied by time and place. I needed content that would work on all of my devices, and that would rely on an internet connection. We'll discuss all of these technology practicalities in Part Two of this book.

B2C example

I'm looking at what I can do with my airline loyalty points, how the process works and where I might like to go. This process is as much about enjoying the process of looking at the destinations I could visit as it is about making any sort of practical plan.

As I work through this process I will make a number of steps that may include, but are not limited to:

- trying to log into my account online to see how many points I have;
- understanding the process of using the points to book flights;
- seeing how far the flights can take me and a list of available destinations, without having a destination in mind;
- understanding when flights are available;

- looking at the destinations, exploring holiday options and looking at the suitability for different types of travel (romantic, family, etc);
- working out the most cost-effective way of using my points considering airport taxes and other charges.

On initial inspection, none of these steps need be mobile-only steps. But also bear in mind I said this was as much about fun as it was about practical planning, so this was most likely to be done when I am relaxing or in between other activities. Therefore, a lot, if not all, of this research would be done on a mobile device from my sofa, office chair or when travelling. Around 30 per cent of all travel bookings are now carried out on mobile devices and at least 60 per cent of travel site traffic is on a mobile device (Criteo, 2016).

I give this example because, not only is it real, but with my particular airline of choice it turned out to be nearly impossible. The key point here is that it was essential to understand the motivation of my user journey, and that was to explore, to learn and to 'mock plan'. Let's take a look at some of the issues that got in the way of this process meeting my requirements:

- main site redirecting to mobile site with limited functionality;
- no ability to go back to main website easily;
- main website not designed to work on multiple devices;
- search options not suited to my user journey, ie being unsure of my final destination;
- no easy way to browse availability without browsing through page after page of dates;
- no further information or recommended sites on potential destinations;
- unclear guidance on travel options when travelling with family (I will not be popular if I'm sitting in business class sipping cocktails and waving to my family back in economy).

These aren't just technology issues. They had an app after all. They just hadn't thought through the different user journeys, and the process had been mapped to work with their booking system rather than the user's needs.

If this journey was embraced, any airline or holiday company I was engaging with would have the opportunity to engage me, reinforce their brand and give me inspiration for future travel. Even if it didn't lead to me booking there and then, by making the process easier they could improve my brand loyalty and potential word-of-mouth recommendations. Instead I'm writing in a book about how frustrating it was!

Local intent

I have so far left out mentioning the consumer with local intent. Not because it isn't important, but because it can be a distraction from the broader picture. If your business has any sort of location-based offering it can be immensely powerful, but this goes back to our concept of understanding the target audience's objectives and context, and then using mobile technologies to deliver the most appropriate solution.

According to Google, 94 per cent of smartphone users have carried out a local search (Think with Google, 2016). If I am looking for a local hotel, my nearest bus stop, a nearby provider of power supplies for my brand of laptop and so on, this type of search is transformational to both the mobile user and potentially any business involved.

We'll explore mobile and retail, where local mobile use can have a huge impact, in the next chapter on integration. We'll also look at mobile search in depth in Part Two and how this fits in with the user journey.

Content marketing

Content marketing is often talked about when looking at an overarching web strategy, but it's also well worth considering when you are thinking about your mobile marketing. Fundamentally, content marketing is about providing useful and engaging content that is suited to the user's journey. Generally, content marketing is about providing value beyond your direct product offering. If we go back to my example of selecting a hosting provider, a useful focus for content marketing would have been educating the user about web technologies.

In Table 2.2 we consider a few more examples.

Table 2.2 Ideas for content marketing themes

Type of company	Focus of content marketing
SEO agency	Digital marketing advice
White water rafting (aimed at teams)	Human resources
Alcoholic drink brand	Cocktail-making and recipes
Detergent	Family money-savings tips
Sportswear	Training tips
Business service	Thought leadership articles

Content marketing, value proposition and mobile

Content marketing allows us to bolster our value proposition through digital-delivered content or services. Mobile specifically allows us to deliver content in a form that is most useful to the audience at the right time. More importantly, we have the opportunity to use mobile technologies creatively to deliver this value proposition via interaction.

Let's take our ideas for content marketing themes, and in Table 2.3 look at how they could be applied in an interactive way. All of these very simple ideas could be developed into something far more robust that would inter-actively reinforce a brand value proposition.

Table 2.3 Content marketing themes and mobile interaction ideas

Focus of content marketing	Interactive idea
Digital marketing advice	Campaign reporting tool
Human resources	Interactive HR guide with scenario planning
Cocktail-making and recipes	Interactive portable recipe book
Family money-savings tips	Coupons and location-based savings
Training tips	Training objective progress tracker
Thought leadership articles	Podcast/audio for learning on the move

It's important to understand how this can be applied to organizations with completely different products or service offerings. A B2B service is generally a high-involvement purchase. That is, you think carefully and do some research before buying. Buying confectionery on the other hand is generally a very low-involvement purchase. You're unlikely to go online and compare chocolate bars before buying them! However, using digital-delivered services and content marketing can help bolster value proposition and brand positioning in both cases.

The stages of the user journey

Any online journey goes through a number of different stages, starting with a lack of awareness about a topic all the way through to direct commercial intent and post-purchase loyalty (or lack of!). There is a wide range of different models that can help us visualize this, but I think considering a traditional sales funnel is a great place to start.

Traditional sales funnel

A traditional sales funnel sees our target audience move from no commercial intent and general browsing or having a vague notion on a topic, through to having an active interest, on to the actual point of purchase and finally into the potential loyalty stage (Figure 2.1).

What the diagram also shows is that this journey is not necessarily a linear one. I may spend an extended period of time browsing and revisiting content before I ever move on to the active interest phase. Also, the duration of the active interest phase will vary according to product/service offering and target audience. Once into the loyalty stage I may also find content intended for the browsing stage useful again as well.

Figure 2.1 The sales funnel

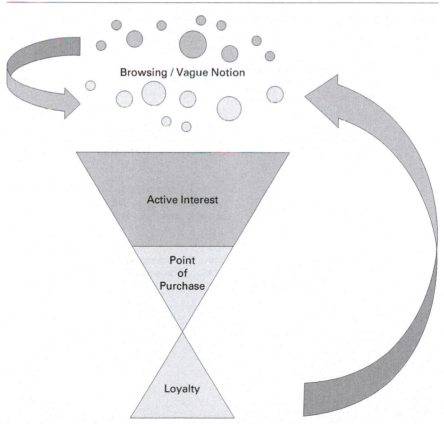

With each stage of the journey I need to understand my target audience's objectives and motivations and work out what content and interactions will drive them to the next stage. We'll look at how we can map content against this funnel in a moment.

See, Think, Do, Care

Avinash Kaushik is a best-selling author, renowned analytics expert and a digital marketing evangelist for Google. Through his excellent blog, Occam's Razor, he has described his very useful See, Think, Do, Care framework (Kaushik, 2016). You can read more about it at http://www.kaushik.net/avinash/, but it is a simple-to-understand yet very flexible and effective model for planning content.

In reality our funnel model and the See, Think, Do, Care framework are actually telling us the same thing. We need different content in different contexts for each stage of the user journey.

Figure 2.2 Avinash Kaushik's See, Think, Do, Care framework

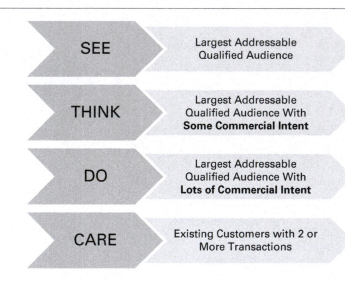

Content mapping

So let's take a couple of examples and look at how we can map content against each of the stages of both user journey models. We'll take two very different organizations: TargetInternet.com, a B2B organization that sells access to online digital marketing courses; and Tesco.com, a global online grocery retailer. Table 2.4 shows the four stages of the user journey (from both user journey models) and then shows examples of content at each stage for a particular audience.

The see/browse content is of broad general interest to our target audience. The think/active interest content is actively related to what the organizations sell. The do/point of purchase content is their key product offering. You'll notice the content at the see/browse stage can also be used at the care/loyalty stage as well.

Table 2.4 User journey models and content mapping

Stage	TargetInternet.com	Tesco.com
See (Browse)	7 top Facebook tips for social success	25 things to do with your children on a rainy day
Think (Active Interest)	Complete guide to bridging the digital marketing skills gap	20 healthy ideas for children's lunch boxes
Do (Point of Purchase)	Online digital marketing courses	Online grocery shopping
Care (Loyalty)	7 top Facebook tips for social success	25 things to do with your children on a rainy day

Value proposition and user journey

Once we map out and understand our different target audiences, their different motivations and the user journeys they could potentially take, we start to have the basis of a digital plan. Once we align this to our business objectives and can measure for success and improvement we have the makings of a digital strategy.

The third and final section of this book will give you a series of checklists to help bring together your digital strategy.

CASE STUDY   Heineken Share the Sofa

Industry

Beverages brand

Agency

Tribal DDB

Location

Global

Marketing objectives

Maximize impact of Champions League sponsorship
Drive brand awareness and engagement
Improve sales

Their challenge

The key insight at the heart of the campaign is that 76 per cent of people watching the Champions League (a European football tournament) were watching it alone at home, and most of them were multi-screening with tablets and smartphones whilst watching the games.

Their solution

The Share the Sofa campaign created hundreds of pieces of video content that were broadcast via Twitter live as the football matches were played. These video clips were made by football celebrities who shared their opinions and insights on the match in a light-hearted and highly visual way from their own sofa.

Their results

The campaign generated over 1.2 billion content views and gave Heineken a 79 per cent share of all conversations in relation to the Champions League sponsorship online. It also led to a 7 per cent increase in purchase intent in the target audience.

What's good about it

It's a great campaign because it takes a clear audience insight on multi-screening and uses this to develop a core creative concept. The campaign was picked up by numerous media outlets and discussed globally, adding to its reach and impact.

Further insights

The campaign used some innovative techniques to achieve live video-streaming because it was created before Periscope (a Twitter app to create live video-streams) was created. Because of Periscope, and other social live video-streaming, such as Facebook Live, these kinds of campaigns are much easier to create now from a technical point of view.

View the case study video:
http://www.targetinternet.com/heineken-share-the-sofa-case-study/.

Technology change and adoption

03

As I have already said, mobile marketing is more about the user journey than it is about the technology. However, we need to understand the adoption of the technology to really understand our target audiences and how we can best reach them. In this chapter we will try and explore and benchmark where the technology currently fits into this puzzle and start to understand the differences between distinct markets and segments of our audience.

Forty years of radical change

At the time of writing it is 43 years since Martin Cooper, a senior engineer at Motorola, made the first mobile phone call on 3 April 1973. Within 10 years they had launched the DynaTAC 8000x (Figure 3.1), their first commercial handheld mobile phone.

Figure 3.1 The DynaTAC 8000x: a snip at $3,995 in 1983

The change in the world of technology and how this has impacted the world of mobile has been radical to say the least. Bear in mind there was no internet when this phone was first in use and that SMS (short messaging service or 'text messaging' as it is often referred to) didn't even get a technical definition until some years later.

The *2016 GSMA Mobile Economy* report found that there were just under 5 billion unique mobile phone subscriptions worldwide. The global population at the time was just over 7 billion (GSM Association, 2016).

Integrated devices

Our expectations of mobile devices are radically different now and smartphones and tablets offer us fully integrated computing and telecommunications devices. This integration is what has led to the radical change in usage that we need to understand in order to make the best use of mobile marketing.

When you consider the level of internet searches done on mobile devices, social media interactions and e-mail reading and writing (all of which we will explore shortly), we quickly see that the device becomes less and less relevant, whilst what we are doing with it becomes far more important.

Smartphone adoption

We could at this point start to look at dozens of charts and facts that wow us with the high level of adoption of mobile phone and smartphone technology (and forgive me, I will do this a little!). In reality, though, smartphone adoption, as a percentage of population, is probably lower than most of us expect (Figure 3.2).

So, if smartphone penetration is actually below 50 per cent, even in highly developed markets like Asia (and even within Asia there are radical variations between regions) why are we getting so excited? Does this mean that this is a minority audience? The answer is actually no.

When you factor in some key demographic data like age, you start to realize that a large percentage of the population is unlikely to own smartphones in the first place. By this I mean young children. According to Index Mundi (who compile their data from the *CIA World Factbook* no less!), in June 2016 around 26.2 per cent of the world population was 0–14 years

Figure 3.2 Smartphone adoption as a percentage of population

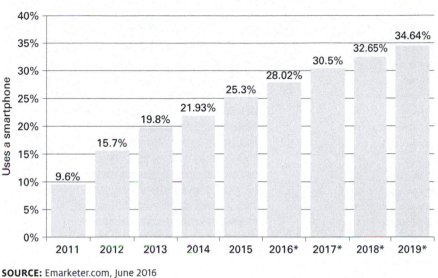

SOURCE: Emarketer.com, June 2016
*predicted

old. Many of this group are unlikely to own a smartphone. However, we will explore this further later, as for example, my daughter was a highly active smartphone user from 11 years old, and my son was using a tablet from the age of two.

Global variations

We also need to be careful to understand the global variations in smartphone adoption and what is causing this (Figure 3.3).

Many of these variations in adoption rates are related to income (smartphones tend to be more expensive than basic 'feature phones') and to geographical coverage offered by the various mobile phone operators that offer data connections.

For example, back in 2013 the three major phone operators in China on average had only 22 per cent 3G data penetration (Jones, 2013). However, by 2016 this figure was expected to reach 80 per cent for 4G penetration (*China Daily*, June 2016)!

Figure 3.3 Smartphone penetration top countries

Rank ≑	Country ≑	% of population owning a smartphone ≑	Relative size ≑
1	South Korea	88	
2	Australia	77	
3	Israel	74	
4	United States	72	
5	Spain	71	
6	United Kingdom	68	
7	Canada	67	
8	Chile	65	
8	Malaysia	65	
10	Germany	60	
10	Italy	60	
12	Turkey	59	
13	China	58	
14	Palestine	57	
15	Lebanon	52	
16	Jordan	51	
17	France	49	
18	Argentina	48	
19	Russia	45	
19	Venezuela	45	
21	Brazil	41	
21	Poland	41	

SOURCE: Pew Research Centre, 2016

Benchmarking marketing activity

Since adoption rates change so quickly and vary so widely by geography, we need reliable sources of data for the regions we are targeting. The following tools offer a range of free insights into mobile usage globally and are updated regularly.

Consumer Barometer

Although the Consumer Barometer is not purely a mobile marketing tool, it is excellent for understanding how mobile makes up part of the overall user journey.

The tool highlights data from 39 countries and looks at how people use the internet to research and buy products (see Figure 3.4). You can explore

Figure 3.4 Consumer Barometer tool

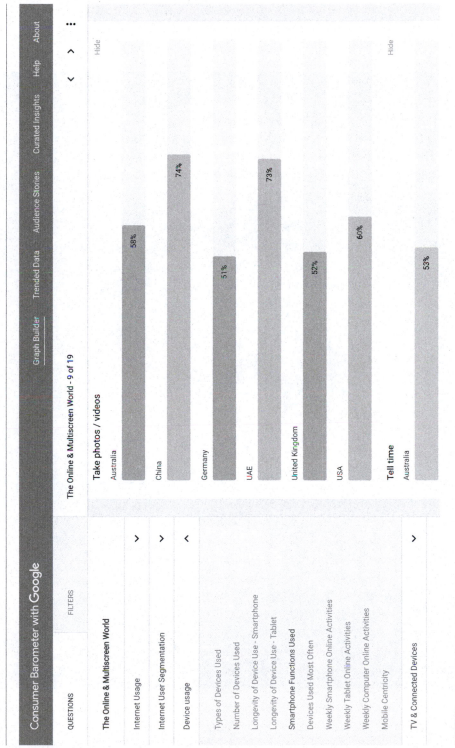

SOURCE: www.consumerbarometer.com

Figure 3.5 Global digital statistics

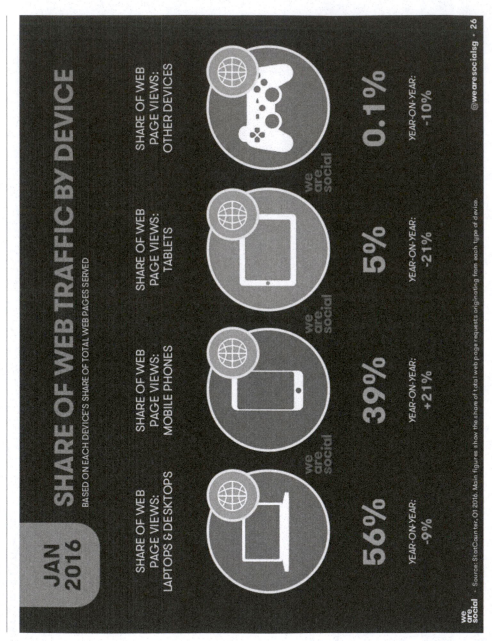

JAN
2016

SHARE OF WEB TRAFFIC BY DEVICE

BASED ON EACH DEVICE'S SHARE OF TOTAL WEB PAGES SERVED

SHARE OF WEB
PAGE VIEWS:
LAPTOPS & DESKTOPS

SHARE OF WEB
PAGE VIEWS:
MOBILE PHONES

SHARE OF WEB
PAGE VIEWS:
TABLETS

SHARE OF WEB
PAGE VIEWS:
OTHER DEVICES

56%

YEAR-ON-YEAR:
-9%

39%

YEAR-ON-YEAR:
+21%

5%

YEAR-ON-YEAR:
-21%

0.1%

YEAR-ON-YEAR:
-10%

we
are
social · Source: StatCounter, Q1 2016. Main figures show the share of total web page requests originating from each type of device.

@wearesocialsg · 26

SOURCE: Digital in 2016, www.wearesocial.com/uk/special-reports/digital-in-2016

the data by browsing around, or by building your own charts as with the Mobile Planet tool.

Digital in 2016 (We Are Social)

This excellent free report (see Figure 3.5) covers a huge range of statistics across digital marketing and looks specifically at mobile adoption and usage across the world. It is broken down into regional reports and is updated several times a year.

For a list of the latest mobile marketing tools and market insights visit: http://www.targetinternet.com/mobilemarketing.

Disruption and integration 04

We have so far examined the mobile consumer and some of the high-level technology issues that have impacted the broad world of mobile marketing. What we haven't done is look in a little more detail at the profound and disruptive effect mobile is already having on some businesses and markets.

Much of this change comes back to our understanding of the user journey, but really it is about convenience, choice and transparency of information for the consumer.

My favourite statistic to demonstrate this is that 65 per cent of shoppers believe they can find better deals via their mobile device (UPS, 2016). In the same report, it shows that single-channel, retail store-only purchases have dropped by 20 per cent (that is, shopping that doesn't include any online element at all but just a visit to a store).

> 65 per cent of shoppers believe they can find better deals via their mobile device.

If we know that people aren't buying because of price, and that they can easily find out that lower prices are available elsewhere, we have a few simple choices. We can compete on price (very difficult in retail), find something else to compete on (like service, quality of experience, value added, etc), or get out of the business before it fails. Painful news for many retailers but true none the less.

This fundamental shift in what retailers need to provide has been caused by the convenience, choice and transparency that mobile, and more broadly, digital marketing gives.

The attitude of many retailers is that if you need something urgently you will still come into the store. This is also being disrupted by digital and smart business. I needed to buy an audio cable for my computer. I knew that my best chance locally was a store called Maplin who always stocked these kinds of products. Not only was the website able to tell me if they had the correct cable in stock, in what stores and how many, they also had smart delivery options. I could get it next day, but more importantly I could get it delivered to my home within 90 minutes (using a smart service called Shutl). Bearing in mind this was cheaper than paying for parking near the store, why would I go in-store?

The death of in-store retail

So does this mean that retail is dead? No, but it means it needs to change and adapt to an environment that has radically changed. People will still go in-store, but for different reasons. It may be for the excellent product advice, great experience, to get hands-on with a product or as a leisure activity. The one thing you can be sure of, though, is that, if you are competing on price, in-store retail is going to be increasingly challenging, unless your store acts as part of a multi-channel approach.

Mobile: the saviour of retail

There is, however, an alternative view to this scenario. It still includes radical change, but envisions mobile as the saviour of in-store retail. Let's consider the concept that we explored in Chapter 2, of using mobile technology to create experiences that bolster the value proposition. There is no reason that mobile can't bolster the value proposition that it's worth going in-store.

By utilizing the appropriate technology, be it apps, near field communication (NFC), beacons or mobile-optimized websites (all of which we'll explore in Part Two), we can improve the in-store retail experience. It may just be that the store experience drives the online sale, but if that is the case we need to understand the user journey to analyse this.

Mobile search can tell me that another online retailer is selling the same product I'm looking at in-store cheaper online. However, it can also tell me that the store I'm in offers better-quality customer service post-sale, a great returns policy and free in-store product training. It may be that by buying in-store I get access to a loyalty programme, or because I've signed up to their app/website I get priority treatment in-store.

For years, airlines and hotels have used loyalty programmes to attract repeat custom from a market that may otherwise be price sensitive. Many of the same principles can be applied to mobile and retail (and many other markets as well).

Convenience, choice and transparency

When we look at markets that have been disrupted by digital technology, the key is to understand why this technology has changed the user experience and journey (or context of the journey).

The media industry has been massively disrupted. Music, film and publishing have all seen massive changes in the delivery of their product. Technology has created a more convenient, flexible and instantaneous delivery channel than ordering a physical product. While there will always be a demand for vinyl and print, the increased convenience, choice and the transparency of pricing meant that the music and publishing industries changed quickly and consumers moved more quickly than media companies. The user experience had changed, massively for the better, and instead of embracing this, the industry dragged its heels. This allowed online piracy to seem like a viable alternative to many who would have paid online, given the option. Over 78 per cent of people are now willing to pay for content online (Williams, 2016).

Business culture

This brings us to a highly important point: that of the culture within an organization. In a fast-paced, rapidly changing environment, which digital and mobile will continue to be for the foreseeable future, we need a culture that allows for change and flexibility. The technology behind mobile marketing in itself is not too complex (or at least I hope you'll think so by the time you read Part Two of this book).

What is complex and generally difficult is change within organizations. Change management has always been challenging, and what mobile marketing is causing is the need for ongoing change. We need to build organizations and organizational cultures that allow for rapid change. In my experience, the bigger the company, the harder this can be.

Single-customer view

One very practical aspect of this is the ability to understand our potential and existing customers better. We have access to more data than ever before (we'll explore this data from mobile apps, advertising and websites in Part Two). As we collect more and more data, though, we need to actually do something with it. It needs to be analysed and actions taken.

Doing something with data

In my experience many companies are now collecting and reporting on web analytics data. What they are not doing is analysing that data in any robust way and actioning that analysis. There is quite often a monthly meeting where a couple of charts are shown, generally looking at volume-based data like 'number of site visits'. The chart is going up, everyone looks happy and the meeting moves on.

This is a huge missed opportunity to learn and improve our digital marketing efforts; data can give us great insight into how effective our mobile marketing actually is. Take a look at Chapter 19 on mobile analytics to learn more about this.

The idea of a single-customer view is a very simple one, but can be extremely difficult to achieve (particularly in larger organizations). The idea is that we connect up the data we get from our mobile apps, websites, e-mail campaigns, social media and so on, build a complete picture of our audience, and are thus able to become smarter marketers. In the best-case scenario, we can connect all of this data to our customer relationship management (CRM) systems and we have a unified and easy way to interrogate sources of information.

Figure 4.1 Achieving a single-customer view

The painful truth about integration

The challenge of integrating data sources is that it is generally a fairly complicated IT project for most organizations. What we are really talking about is database, third-party supplier and legacy systems integration, and what this means in reality is complexity. However, it doesn't need to be this way.

If I am a small business, it's a different picture. I can get some form of web analytics like Google Analytics, a cloud-based CRM system like SalesForce, and various systems like MailChimp (an online e-mail service provider (ESP)). All of these will 'plug in' to one another with not too much effort, and I have a relatively effective single-customer view.

Even in large organizations, by carefully selecting suppliers with a single-customer view in mind, I can work toward this ideal scenario step by step. We may not be able to integrate all data immediately, but this should be our long-term objective.

Next step: marketing automation

Marketing automation is something that is most often used in the B2B world, but it can be applied to almost any industry, product or service to some extent. The core principle is that if I have insight into your behaviour on a single or multiple channels, I can automatically trigger relevant communications to you at the right time.

At its most simple level, imagine getting a push notification via an app some time after you have made a purchase, asking for a review. This is a basic form of marketing automation.

At its more advanced level I can start to 'score' your behaviour across multiple platforms to try and identify particular types of customers, potential leads or customers who are having problems finding the right information.

The B2B world tends to be well suited to marketing automation due to the long sales times, involved buying process, multiple touch points before purchase and high value of a sale. It can also be applied to consumer goods if tied in with digital services that are there to bolster value proposition. For example, a sportswear manufacturer can track your behaviour through an app that monitors your fitness goals and triggers relevant communications at the right time.

Mobile as a change enabler

So we've looked at how mobile technology can be disruptive, but also how this can actually be a change for good by improving the customer experience and can lead to improved awareness, engagement and loyalty in the long term. By fully exploiting the technology available in a way that embraces the increased convenience, choice and transparency available to the mobile consumer, we can mitigate risk and maximize opportunity.

CASE STUDY Digital Marketing podcast

Topic

Mobile disruption

Industry

Automotive

Expert

Ciaran Rogers, host of the Digital Marketing podcast

Tapping into the brave new mobile frontier

Driverless cars will soon be a reality, with Google, Apple and a host of large car manufacturers all joining the development race to have the first fully automated vehicle available to buy by 2020 or sooner. But are society and the car manufacturing industry really ready for them and the complete overhaul of the automotive industry they will inevitably bring?

It won't just be a revolution in how the car drives and navigates. That's the obvious change. It's the interesting knock-on effects in what consumers will demand from their cars once the car can drive itself that are fascinating. Think about it... If the car no longer needs a driver, then one of the core requirements around which cars have been designed for the last 110 years just changed. There won't be a requirement for the driver to see from all angles and to be in control at all times. There will be no requirement to ensure the driver is free from distraction with their eyes upon the road. In fact, for passengers (and everyone in these vehicles will be passengers) the interesting revolution will occur around what those passengers choose to rest their eyes and ears upon.

Time is a key factor here (or rather the lack of it). In the UK on average we typically spend an estimated 10 hours a week driving (*The Telegraph*, 2016). That's largely dead time for the driver and little better for passengers in terms of what you can do productively during transit. Based around current standard car designs, self-driving cars would simply boost our opportunity to watch the world go by. Fine for short journeys in picturesque surroundings – but seriously, for most car journeys? In-car entertainment is going to be key, and that will require a great deal of creativity and imagination from car manufacturers because in-car entertainment is likely to be the key feature that differentiates the must-have driverless vehicle from all the other driverless drones in the market.

To date much of the tech on offer relies on use of mobile phones or tablets within the car space, but given that the layout of a driverless vehicle can be what you want it to be, larger shared screens that offer a more immersive experience and don't have to be self-powered are a real option.

Driverless cars have the potential to further extend what the mobile phone and standard living-room tech offers consumers today. An extension of our real-world and online self, but with a way better battery life and an amazingly immersive screen! With other technological shifts currently taking place it is entirely possible that virtual reality and augmented reality will all play their part in the active revisualization of the 10 hours a week of clear space that will potentially open up for those who inhabit these autonomous vehicles. And perhaps it is this frontier of untapped time that has all the tech giants of the world scrabbling to enter into the automobile arena.

Tech giants such as Google and Apple fully understand how hard it is to reach large audiences in a distraction-free environment. They have built complex ecosystems to hook users into their channels and in doing so are reaping big rewards from ad and product-related revenues. It makes you wonder if the car manufacturers really appreciate the true value of the time frontier they are about to open up. What is the true value of millions of people's time and attention for seven–eight hours a week? Google and Apple will be well aware. Volvo Ford and Toyota? I'm not so sure. It isn't their business… yet. They make cars, right? Well, they did, but in less than five years they have the opportunity to be in command of one of the gateways to this untapped time frontier if Apple and Google don't steal the markets right from under their retro-styled bonnets.

The car OS that powers the autonomous vehicle and its digital communications and entertainment systems has the potential to net regular ongoing monthly income throughout the life of the car, and the manufacturers are the gatekeepers to the whole market. Forget Android vs Apple iOS updates; car OS updates and upgrades could soon become the tech industry's most talked-about summer and winter releases. Top that with your car's mobile internet connectivity and you have a whole new category of options and sales to explore. Music-streaming, video-streaming, voice and video-calling solutions are all there to be chosen, partnered with and packaged. It's game-changing and mind-boggling when you start to think about it, and as none of these cars are actually in production yet, for the manufacturers who embrace the golden opportunities this new trend will open there is still all to play for.

Devices, platforms and technology

Why it doesn't matter

It's easy to get bogged down in working out which mobile devices your app should work on, what happens when a new phone version comes out and how effective your responsive design website is (all of which we explore in detail in Part Two). All of this stuff matters because of the final outcome of your mobile campaigns, but the reality is that your mobile consumers don't care. They just want to be able to get stuff done.

Responsive design means absolutely nothing to the majority of the people on this planet (and maybe to you right now) and nor should it. I don't really care how my house was built as long as it keeps me dry, warm and secure. However, if my house doesn't work when it rains, or when the sun shines, I will have a serious problem with the builders.

You need to worry about the technical aspects of your mobile strategy but your users should not. They shouldn't even notice it.

Mobile-compatible is not mobile-optimized

Just because your website works on mobile devices does not mean it is mobile-optimized. What I mean is that the site may load up fine on my phone, but if I have to zoom in a dozen times to see anything clearly, this isn't an optimal experience.

We'll explore the ins and outs of building mobile sites in Part Two, but what we need to consider now is what my target audience is likely to do, in what context and on what devices. I can then start to make sure I have ticked the appropriate boxes to make their experience as pain-free as possible.

Users are even more impatient on mobile devices than they are when using a desktop or laptop (Work, 2011). They have come across so many poor mobile sites they just give up very quickly. On the other hand, if we can create a seamless mobile experience we stand a better chance of achieving our objectives and can actually build loyalty.

Technology challenges

So, you're thinking something along the lines of 'It's all very good saying the technology doesn't matter, but I have to make choices and every time I make a change it costs money.' You're 100 per cent right. The reality is this has always been the case in marketing. We have to decide where to spend our money and how to prioritize our budgets. The actual problem here is that the number of options is large and we don't ask the right questions.

Asking the right questions

Rather than asking whether you should build an Android, iOS or a Black-berry app (if you have no idea what I'm talking about, take a look at the box opposite), we should actually be asking what devices your target audience uses and which groups will it be most cost effective to reach. Let's frame this for a moment by forgetting about mobile. If I decide I am targeting an audience but can only afford to target half of it, I need to decide which half. I don't do this based on an opinion; I should most likely do it on the potential lifetime value of those customers, how much it will cost to target them and other commercially focused criteria. The same applies to the different mobile platforms and choices we make within our mobile strategies.

Platform wars

We'll explore the technical side of mobile sites and apps in Part Two, but it's worth understanding the key players in the mobile operating system (OS) market. For the sake of simplicity, we've just looked at the major smartphone and tablet platforms here. An OS is just the software that a phone runs on and will impact its functionality. Most importantly for us, apps built for one platform generally don't work on another. We'll look at these in more detail later.

Android

Google's mobile OS. It's open source, meaning it can theoretically be used and adapted by anyone. It has also been adopted by the Open Handset Alliance (OHA) which includes big handset manufacturers such as Samsung, Sony and HTC.

iOS

Apple's OS, used on its iPhone, AppleTV and iPad products range. It is closely associated with OS X used on Apple Mac computers.

Blackberry

Blackberry's OS for all Blackberry devices.

Windows Mobile

Microsoft's OS is used on their Lumia phones and is an iteration of their main PC operating system.

Beyond these platforms with the largest market share there are a whole lot more. Take a look at Wikipedia to see just how many – and then don't worry about them! (By the way, if you are going to send me hate mail about telling people to ignore your particular mobile OS of choice, you should probably get out more.) http://wikipedia.org/wiki/Mobile_operating_system.

Audience segmentation

Just because 40 per cent of the world uses a particular type of mobile OS, it doesn't mean that your target audience in your target market does. For this reason, you shouldn't rely on a lot of the generalized statistics that are published.

In reality, your target audience probably won't necessarily align with the norms of your overall market, and if you're working across multiple regions it clearly gets more complicated. What we really need to do is to collect some actual market insights as we should with any other aspect of our marketing. You can do this by sample surveying your target audience and actually asking the question.

Frictionless technology

What we are aiming for is to make the process of achieving the consumer's goal as simple and as transparent as possible. This idea of making the process as seamless as possible is often referred to as 'frictionless technology' and it's something we'll consider throughout Part Two. What we should always consider in our mobile marketing is what is the objective of the user and how can that most effectively be achieved using the right technology in the right place.

The future of mobile marketing

No book on mobile would be complete without considering the future of the technology and industry. My main thought on this is that the future is a lot closer than we think!

Exponential development

One of the main drivers in the development of mobile marketing is the exponential growth of computing power. As computing power increases and devices get physically smaller, so what our mobile devices can do becomes more and more interesting. Advances like better voice recognition, augmented reality (AR) and high-resolution video displays have all relied on these increases in computing power to make them available on mainstream mobile devices.

Enter Moore's Law

Moore's Law is an often quoted, but quite often not fully understood, observation in regard to the exponential growth of computing power made back in 1965. Gordon E Moore, co-founder of Intel, observed that the number of transistors on integrated circuits doubled roughly every two years.

These changes have a direct impact on the speed at which computers can process information, how much storage they can have in a given space, and are even connected to things like the potential resolution of your digital camera.

This means that computing power grows at an exponential rate (more on that later).

Moore's Law has proved to be exceptionally accurate; although he originally predicted that it would hold true for around 10 years, it has now done so for nearly 50 years.

The future of Moore's Law

There has been much discussion about the fact that Moore's Law cannot continue to hold true forever. Practically speaking, you can only get so many transistors in a physical space before you get to the limit of what is possible due to the limitations of physics.

However, if you look at Moore's Law more broadly, and think in terms of computing power, rather than transistors, there is a clear argument in favour of it holding true. What generally happens, when one technology reaches the limits of what can be done with it, is that some form of innovation is found to continue the progress of technology. Whether that's an entirely new material, manufacturing process or brand new technology, there are lots of examples of innovation allowing Moore's Law to continue when it looked to be reaching its limits.

Exponential growth in perspective

One of the most important elements of this growth in computing power that is impacting our mobile devices is its exponential rate. The human brain is very good at understanding things that grow in a linear way, that is, something that grows at the same rate on an ongoing basis, like counting from 1 to 100. What we are not so good at is getting our heads around exponential growth. The best way to do this is to consider an example.

I first heard the following analogy from my friend, and expert digital strategist, Jonathan Macdonald (look up some of his talks for some real inspiration on the future of technology on his blog at http://ten.io/vault/blogs/). I have seen a number of different versions of the analogy online, but the key thing is to take note at the end of the story.

Filling a stadium with water, one drop at a time

Imagine a large stadium filling with water from a tap, one drip per minute, and imagine that stadium to be watertight so that no water could escape. If the tap continued dripping water in the same regular (linear) way, it would take many thousands of years to fill the stadium.

However, if that tap was dripping at an exponential rate, so that the number of drips coming out of the tap doubled every minute, it's a very different story. The first minute there is one drop, the second minute there are two drops, the third minute four drops, the fourth minute eight drops and so on. This is exponential growth in action.

Now imagine you are sitting on the seat at the very top of the stadium, with a view across the entire area. The first drop from the exponential tap is dropped right in the middle of the stadium field, at 12 noon. Remembering that this drop grows exponentially by doubling in size every minute, how much time do you have to leave the stadium before the water reaches your seat at the very top? Is it hours, days, weeks, months or years?

The answer is that you have exactly until 12.49 pm. It takes an exponential tap less than 50 minutes to fill a whole stadium with water. This is impressive but it gets more interesting. At what time do you think the football stadium is still 93 per cent empty? The answer: at 12.45 pm. So if you sat and watched the water level growing, after 45 minutes all you would see is the stadium field covered with water. Then, within four more minutes, the water would fill the entire stadium. It would then take one more minute to fill an entire other stadium. Exponential growth gets very big, very quickly.

Technology as an enabler

So let's consider what this growth in technology means in practical terms. It means that the devices we use will be able to do more and more things that previously seemed impossible, and the rate of these technology developments will get faster and faster.

You only have to look at technology development over the few decades to see this in practice. Thirty years or so ago, my iPhone would have looked like science fiction. (It should be noted, however, I still don't have a hover car.)

Recent innovations, such as real-time voice recognition language translation or controlling the playback of video by just looking at your device (both innovations used Samsung devices) will seem like common technology in the near future.

This means that the increase in capabilities of the devices we use will enable us to do new things that we won't be currently thinking about. It is also likely that the role a mobile device currently takes in bridging the gap between the physical world and the online world will continue and grow.

The near future

Microsoft's HoloLens product (see Figure 6.1) is a glimpse of a very near future where AR is commonplace. The product is already in existence and Microsoft, as well as external developers, are building and refining what it will be able to do.

Although HoloLens takes fairly widely available technologies, combines them and then wraps them in some clever software, it is causing a major reaction. This is in part due to the clever use of technology, but more about the idea of wearing technology and the idea of being 'constantly connected' and altering the reality around us.

Whenever I show HoloLens to a room full of students, delegates on a training course or an audience at a larger presentation, the audience seems to be divided between two points of view. One group of people is excited

Figure 6.1 Microsoft HoloLens: augmented reality wearable technology

SOURCE: www.microsoft.com/microsoft-hololens/

by the possibilities and impressed by the technology. The other group finds the prospect and implications of being able to change the reality around you disturbing.

Mobile changing society

This reaction is interesting for many reasons, but most of all it shows how mobile technology is changing our day-by-day lives so fundamentally. Essentially, the technology is moving more quickly than society is adapting to it and developing cultural norms in how to deal with it.

I see a great example of this every time I talk at a conference. A few years ago, if I was speaking on stage and somebody was looking down at their phone, it was a sign that I didn't have their attention. This may have been due to my talk being boring, them having more important things to deal with, or the fact that they weren't really interested in the first place. Now when I speak at a conference most people are looking down at their phones. It may be that I am getting increasingly boring, but based on the level of tweets and social media posts, what they are actually doing is broadcasting snippets from my talk in real time.

Double-edged sword

This change in behaviour has both good and bad sides. First, it's great because it means the members of the audience think there is value in what I am saying, enough value in fact to share it with their own, wider audience. That means in turn that I have a wider audience and will gain a larger social media following myself.

The downside is that it means the audience isn't fully listening to what I'm saying and their engagement with my content may be fairly superficial: looking for sound-bites of content to publish.

This double-edged sword is a reflection of two issues in my opinion. First, we haven't developed a culture around these kinds of circumstances yet to have worked out what is the best pattern of behaviour. Secondly, the technology is still getting in the way.

The ideal solution is not only a cultural one, where known behaviour is expected (for example, you turn your mobile off or to silent in the cinema), but also one of better technology. Technology that didn't require me to look down at my mobile device and use my hands to interact with it would mean that posting social media updates would be far less interruptive.

Making things easier

Reducing how much the technology gets in the way of what I am trying to do and creating a more seamless experience is what 'frictionless' technology is all about. We could compare what technology we need to carry now to create, edit and publish a video. Twenty years ago it would have meant a lot of heavy and very expensive equipment. Now it means carrying the average smartphone.

The reaction HoloLens has created because of its wearable nature and the fact that it overlays something onto our 'real world' will become more and more relevant in the very near future. As mobile technology develops, the device itself becomes less and less relevant, and the utility it offers has the opportunity to be more and more frictionless.

Some fairly obvious examples come to mind very easily if you just look at HoloLens. Once the technology gets in the way less, how about not needing a headset at all? How long will it be until we have augmented reality (AR) contact lenses?

How about taking the experience of watching somebody on stage giving a presentation and trying to make the follow-up actions simpler? Using facial recognition, you could automatically be shown the speaker's online profile, previous work and other similar experts. Another example scenario could be that you have gone for a walk in the woods and see a snake. Your AR contact lenses could identify the snake, take a picture and post it to your social networks to share your experience, and most importantly, tell you if it's dangerous or not.

The point is that it's so easy to think of a thousand day-to-day experiences that could be enhanced in some way by using these kinds of technologies. And all of these changes in our everyday experiences will mean that mobile technology becomes more and more personal. You only have to have lost your phone once to realize that we are increasingly reliant and connected to the devices we use.

Privacy and the future of mobile

The overlap between mobile marketing, search and social media is creating circumstances where questions of privacy are increasingly being discussed and challenged.

One of the key features demonstrated in an early Google Glass (Google's original AR glasses) promotion video (which actually showed a mockup of its expected functionality rather what it could actually do at that time) was the wearer of the device asking where his friend was, and his friend's location being immediately shown on the augmented reality display. This particular piece of functionality was always the one that seemed to draw the biggest gasps from an audience because of the implications this could have on privacy. The reality is that smartphone-based geographic location data has been around for some time, but its usage is one of the many things about sharing so much data that is increasingly concerning people.

The key issue at play is that of value exchange and transparency. If I share data with you, am I fully aware of that fact and do I know what you will do with that data? The other question, which consumers are increasingly asking, is: what do you offer me in exchange?

A clear value exchange proposition is going to become increasingly important when we attempt any form of mobile marketing. If I give you my data, what functionality, or other value, will you give me in exchange? Then finally, and most importantly, do I trust you enough to give you my data?

The distant future

Really this section should be entitled 'The seems distant, but will actually probably be a lot sooner than we think, future'. It's not all that catchy, though, so we'll stick with 'distant future'. If we go back to the exponential growth analogy of filling a stadium with water, we can see that the rate of change got pretty radical pretty quickly.

This could mean some very significant changes to the world around us. A very clear point, in my opinion, is the idea that 'mobile technology' will become irrelevant (and some would argue it already is). The integration of technology into everything we do, and even into us as human beings, will mean that the funny little devices we carry around now will in the future seem like the Dark Ages do to us now.

Consider that it's a fairly logical train of thought, that we will all be constantly connected to the internet (whatever that looks like then!), wherever we go. It's also not unreasonable to think that computing power and artificial intelligence will have radically advanced and machines will be far more 'intelligent'. (When you start to consider that sentient life may not be limited to organic organisms, we start to get a little too science fiction for the remit of this book, I'm afraid.) It's also a fairly logical path that would lead us to think we can control and interact with devices by thinking, since you can already get games that allow you to use your brain waves to control physical objects (Fallon, 2009).

These relatively logical progressions of technology mean that the world we live in will be radically changed. I find this extremely exciting and feel very blessed to live in such fast-changing times. If, however, this all fills you with a sense of dread, bear in mind it's the application not the technology that's the issue. When video cassettes first came into usage by the general population, there were huge concerns about 'video nasties'. We adjusted and the world continued.

A guaranteed future prediction

The only guarantee is that the pace of change within the arena of digital technology, and the rate at which this impacts our organizations and wider society, will get faster and faster. Organizations (and individuals) that are able to adapt to ongoing change will be best placed to survive and thrive in this environment.

Let's get practical

And now we move from the future of artificial intelligence and controlling technology with your mind, to the slightly more practical aspects of mobile marketing. Part Two of this book is your hands-on guide to implementing mobile marketing in the real world.

PART TWO
The tactical toolkit

Introduction   07

Part Two of the book is a practical guide to each of the key technologies and practical challenges involved with mobile marketing. It has been written so that you can either read it progressively (just like a normal book), but also as a reference that can be dipped into and out of in the order that is most appropriate to your current challenges.

However, I would advise you to try and learn about all of the aspects of mobile marketing, even if the particular topic or technology doesn't seem relevant for your current situation. Increasingly, the practicalities of technologies involved have an impact on one another and should make up part of an integrated campaign.

Also look out for the highlighted boxes of content. These contain additional information, examples and practical tips that can help save you time and stress when implementing your digital campaigns.

Latest techniques and best practice

Don't forget that you can find examples of the latest mobile marketing techniques, tools and best practice on our website. You can also ask me questions directly and share your experiences: http://www.targetinternet. com/mobilemarketing/.

Mobile sites and responsive design

08

Let's make something clear from the outset; you need a mobile-optimized site. That doesn't mean your site happens to work on mobile devices. It means the user journey via mobile has been carefully considered and you offer the optimal experience via mobile devices. It means that you have weighed up the different technical solutions in order to achieve this and have selected the most appropriate approach. It also means that you have not been steered by the limitations of your current web platform or content management system (CMS).

In this chapter we'll explore why a mobile site really is absolutely essential, why apps and mobile sites aren't a one-or-the-other choice, and how you can achieve your marketing and business objectives using mobile sites.

Start with the fundamentals

Already, over 50 per cent of visitors to many sites get there via mobile devices (Sterling, 2016). This means that, potentially, the majority of your audience will be on a mobile device. This is reason enough to make sure your site is fully optimized for these visitors, before you even consider the potential of increased conversion rates and average order values via a properly optimized mobile experience. Increases in conversion rates of up to 76 per cent have been demonstrated through properly optimized mobile experience (Monetate, 2016).

Focus on the user journey

The key point of a mobile-optimized site is to offer an experience that best suits the consumers' needs and circumstances. This means they should be able to access the information or utility that your site offers, on the device they are using, in an easy and efficient way.

Classic mistakes

Mobile-compatible

Having a website that works on mobile devices often confuses people into thinking they have a mobile-optimized experience. If your website works on mobile devices, but the consumer spends much of his or her time zooming in and out to see anything clearly, this is not an optimized experience.

Broken journey

Adopting the latest technology trends without considering the impact they have on the user journey is a common mistake. Placing a Quick Response (QR) code onto your latest outdoor advertising campaign, without considering the fact that the website you are sending mobile users through to does not work on mobile devices, is not a great idea.

Mobile site dead end

This is my pet hate. It involves visiting a website on a mobile device and then being redirected to a mobile-specific version of the website. Nothing disastrous so far, but there is nothing more annoying than finding the piece of content I need isn't on their mobile site, but their technology won't let me visit their standard site on my mobile device. Every time I try and visit the main site it just redirects me. Give people an option to visit the standard website. Please.

Mobile site options

One size fits all

The first, simplest and least likely to work approach! The idea is that you create one site that works well on desktop and mobile devices. In reality, it normally means that some sacrifices have to be made and that either your desktop or mobile site will need to suffer.

The only scenario in which this really works is when your site is very simple and limited in its functionality. An example of this would be a site based on a single landing page with a sign-up form.

What we are really doing in this scenario quite often is tweaking a website so it at least functions correctly on a mobile device. This clearly isn't a mobile-optimized site, but it may be what you need to do as an interim measure.

What this highlights is that we need to start by understanding what should be the key differences between a mobile and desktop experience and why. We'll explore this in the next section of this chapter.

Dedicated mobile site

A mobile-specific version of your website can seem like the most obvious solution. Basically, you have two versions of your website, a mobile and a desktop version, and depending on the device the site visitor is using, they are given a different version of your site.

You could in fact have multiple versions beyond a desktop and a mobile version, and have versions for individual devices or maybe just separate desktop, smartphone and tablet versions.

The advantage of this approach is the ability to completely adjust a site for an optimized mobile experience. The downside is that you have multiple sites to manage and this can create a few challenges.

The level of complexity this creates will depend on how you update and manage the content of your sites. Static sites, which are sites that are updated and edited by changing the code itself (using a developer or updating it yourself), just mean increased workloads as you have multiple sites to update. Content-managed sites, which are sites where you have some form of interface that allows you to update your site, can be more complex.

CMS can be used in a number of different ways to manage mobile sites:

- **A CMS-based desktop site and static mobile site** – this means you have a mobile-optimized site built but in order to edit and change it, you will need to use a developer or edit the code directly yourself.

- **A CMS-based desktop site and separate CMS for your mobile site** – this means you will have two separate CMSs in order to update the different versions of your sites. This makes the movement of content between the two sites more complex, but can be a fairly straightforward solution.

- **A single CMS for multiple versions of your site** – this means that although you have a separate mobile-optimized site, you are able to manage your site content for multiple sites under one CMS. Generally, this solution will allow you to edit content and 'assign' it to a particular version of your site. This is a fairly elegant solution but requires a CMS that is designed to manage this kind of situation.

Responsive design

Responsive design, sometimes referred to as adaptive design (although these definitions actually mean different things that we'll discuss later), means developing one site that will display appropriately for each device it is viewed on. This means the site can look completely different on each device and will lay out in the way best suited to a particular environment.

This approach is generally implemented using a combination of web technologies like cascading style sheets (CSS) and JavaScript which we'll discuss more in a moment. The key point is that these technologies allow the browser to look at things such as the device the site visitor is using, the width and height of the display, and then decide on how the page should be laid out. Figure 8.1 shows the Target Internet website, and how responsive design can be used effectively. On the left is the full width version, on the right the same site with the browser width reduced. You'll notice, not only is the design made narrower, but the functionality adapts to the new size.

Responsive vs adaptive design

Responsive design and adaptive design are often terms that are used interchangeably; however, they are quite distinct things.

Responsive design is something that is actioned within your browser. This means that a page is sent to your browser, and your browser then does the work to display the correct elements of the page. This is called a client-side technology (the client is your browser).

Adaptive design is something that is actioned on the web server. The type of device being used is identified and then the appropriate version of the site is delivered. This is called a server-side technology.

The advantage of adaptive design is that not as much content is sent to the browser where it may not be used and a solely mobile version of a site is sent to a mobile device. (See the next box on responsive design and its limitations.)

Figure 8.1 Effective responsive sites

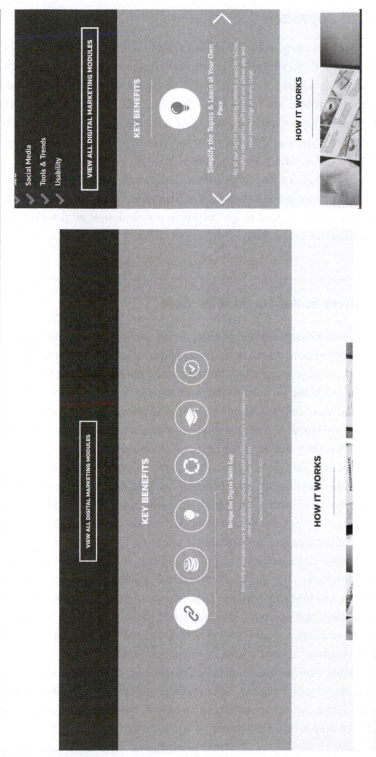

Hybrid approach

There are also some solutions that take elements of dedicated mobile sites and combine them with some responsive design elements. For example, your site could use a number of CSSs to make your site look different on different devices, but your CMS could allow you to select which pages, menu options and other features display on different versions of your site. This essentially amounts to a dedicated mobile site but can help minimize the management time involved in having multiple sites.

There are also other technologies that can be combined with responsive design to get past its limitations and to create an optimized mobile experience. These are often referred to as 'responsive web design with server-side components' or RESS for short.

A silver bullet for mobile sites

Responsive design is often seen as a silver bullet solution, solving all of our mobile site problems. It certainly can offer a single site solution, meaning that your website adapts according to the device of the visitor. There are, however, some considerations you need to be aware of.

First, you need to consider if a responsively designed site can go far enough to really implement a mobile-optimized experience, or whether you are still making compromises because of the limitations of the technology. It's certainly possible to achieve an optimized experience in most scenarios, but this very much depends on how your site is implemented and what functionality you require. In many cases, for example, e-commerce sites still need a dedicated mobile site as responsive design just doesn't give enough flexibility to adapt the site as much as is required.

Another consideration should be load time. If responsive design is implemented poorly, you can end up loading a full desktop site to a mobile device, and then just displaying certain elements of it. For this reason, it is generally a better bet to start considering responsive design from the outset of a web project rather than trying to bolt it on afterwards, as this often leads to 'bloated' websites that can be slow to load.

Rather than being a silver bullet, responsive design techniques are just that: techniques. They can certainly help you achieve a mobile-optimized experience, but you should also be aware of their limitations and that they can be used in combination with other techniques.

Mobile design principles: mobile sites vs desktop sites

So let's take a look in the following section at the key considerations when we are considering mobile sites and the main differences from a desktop version of a website.

Prioritization of content

One of the key issues with mobile devices is generally their screen size and the fact that screens are smaller than those of a desktop or laptop computer. This means that page 'real estate' is at a premium and we need to make viewing and understanding the content as easy as possible.

This generally means considering the mobile user's journey and prioritizing content according to their potential needs. It also means filtering out content that may not be essential in order to de-clutter the mobile experience.

Horizontal vs vertical layout

Smartphones are generally used initially in vertical layout as are tablet devices. Screens on desktop devices, however, are generally horizontally orientated. This orientation needs to be factored into our designs, but we also need to consider the fact that mobile devices can change orientation.

Links and buttons

Throughout websites we use hyperlinks extensively, and hyperlinks are just linked text. This approach is less effective on mobile devices because of the size of screens relative to our input device, ie our fingers. For this reason, buttons tend to work better on mobile devices but can look extremely clunky on desktop sites.

Screen size and graphics

Quite clearly we are generally dealing with smaller screen sizes and we have already discussed how screen space is at a premium. However, this lack of space and screen size mean that many graphics that are suitable for desktop-based sites are not suitable on mobile sites. This is generally due to the lack of clarity when an image is small and because of the amount of space they are taking up in the precious amount of space available.

Reduced hierarchy

Many desktop-based sites offer various ways of navigating their content, hierarchical menu systems and page elements like breadcrumb trails that show where you are on the site. Because of space limitations we often need to remove many of these elements. However, it is also essential that the mobile user does not feel lost or confused as to where they are on the site. For this reason, having a reduced and simpler hierarchy on your mobile site can make things much easier.

Phone integration

Phones clearly have additional functionality not offered by desktop devices that can often be used within mobile sites (apps can generally access these functionalities even more effectively and we'll discuss that in Chapter 10 on apps later). Things like geographic location, click-to-maps, click-to-text and so on can be utilized to improve the mobile experience.

Technology and jargon in perspective

When talking about mobile site development, there are a lot of technical terms and technologies involved. Below you'll find a few of the most important ones that should help you navigate, discuss and develop your mobile site plans:

- HTML – hypertext markup language (HTML) is the markup language used to lay out web pages. The files sent to our web browsers when we request a web page are HTML files which are then translated by the browser into what we see.
- CSS – cascading style sheets (CSS) describes the styling information for a markup language. This basically means it defines what different parts of a web page should look like. A range of CSS can be used on different devices to generate varying content layout.
- JavaScript – JavaScript is a client-side language (meaning it is run and used within a browser) to add extra functionality to web pages. It is often used to help select which is the most appropriate CSS to use on a particular device.

- **Responsive design** – responsive design allows web pages to be displayed differently on different devices by adjusting the layout and page elements shown. These adjustments are made within the browser.

- **Adaptive design** – adaptive design allows for a specific version of a web page to be sent to a specific device or browser. Once the device and/or browser is known, only the relevant version of the web page is sent to the browser.

- **Progressive enhancement** – this is an approach to building web pages that tries to prevent sending content to basic browsers that wouldn't be compatible with it. This means a basic version of a web page is built and then gradually enhanced for more sophisticated browsers. The more sophisticated elements of the page are not loaded initially, meaning there is no wasted load time.

- **RESS** – responsive web design with server-side components (RESS) is a technique combining elements of responsive web design and other technologies to maximize the mobile experience and bypass shortcomings of individual techniques. RESS is also often referred to as 'adaptive design'.

- **Media queries** – these are part of CSS and an important part of responsive design. They allow the layout to adapt to the screen resolution and layout.

- **Fluid grid** – the fluid grid principle is that web pages should be positioned and laid out according to percentages rather than fixed sizes and positions. This means that layouts can more easily be adapted for different sizes of screens.

Mobile site and responsive design examples

For some great examples of mobile sites and to see responsive design in practice, visit our website: http://www.targetinternet.com/mobilemarketing.

What responsive design really means

When many people talk about responsive design, they are in fact talking about using a number of different technologies to achieve an optimal mobile experience. These differing ways of using the same phrase is why you'll find so much discussion online about the pros and cons of responsive design.

In reality, when most people talk about responsive design they are actually talking about a number of techniques working together and are actually referring to RESS techniques or other hybrid solutions.

The three-step quick and dirty guide to a responsive website

I wish somebody had given me the following advice at the beginning of my digital marketing career as it would have saved me lots and lots of pain in building websites from scratch, on bespoke CMS, and wrangling over expensive functionality improvements to my sites.

This is not supposed to be a thorough website specification building process, and in fact it ignores nearly all of the key steps I would normally go through in order to get a professional website built. It ignores usability principles, mapping the user journey, content auditing and a million other key and valid principles. What it does do, though, is demonstrate how quickly you actually get a responsive site up and running. Whether that site will deliver on your marketing objectives is a different question!

All behold the mighty WordPress!

Let us be absolutely clear that I love WordPress. I think it is one of the best things that has ever happened to the web and I am unapologetically enthusiastic about it! The simple reason is that it makes building many types of websites quick, easy and cost effective. This includes mobile websites and using responsive design.

WordPress started out as an open source (meaning it is free to use) blogging platform. It is still a blogging platform, but in reality it is a highly flexible CMS capable of building and managing websites of most types – and it's free. In fact, more than one in four of the world's websites are built on WordPress (W3Techs, 2016)!

If you go to WordPress.com you can set up a WordPress blog and have it up and running in minutes. This blog will be hosted by WordPress and you will have a vast, but slightly limited, set of capabilities to build websites.

The alternative approach, and one that we are discussing here, is to go to WordPress.org (see Figure 8.2) where the software can be downloaded and installed onto your own servers and customized as much as needed. You can do this yourself if you have the technical skills (see the box on page 72 on the kind of skills you'll need and that are worth having).

Figure 8.2 WordPress software

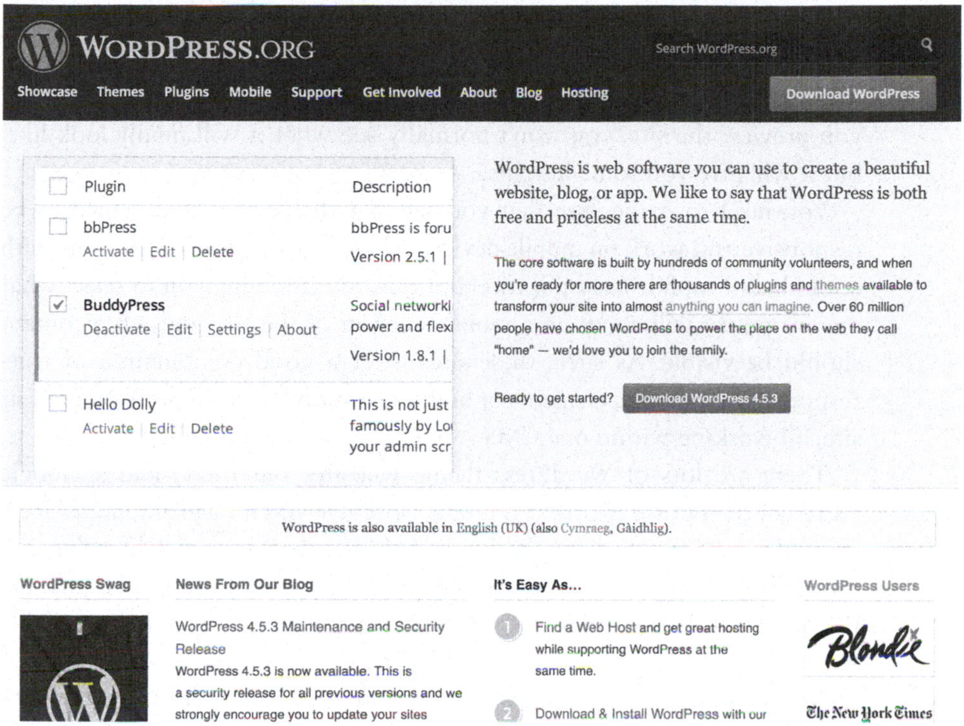

SOURCE: www.wordpress.org

Step 1: Get some hosting

You're going to need some hosting space online that is capable of hosting WordPress. This hosting will generally require two things: the ability to process PHP, the language in which WordPress is written; and the ability to have a database, so you'll need MySQL on the server as well.

Before you run away in panic, as this is all starting to sound quite technical, lots of hosting companies have packages designed specifically for WordPress hosting and many come with it pre-installed. WordPress even give you a guide to hosting and recommend some companies (see http://wordpress.org/hosting/).

Step 2: Select a responsive theme

WordPress uses something called 'themes' to customize the look and feel of your site. This is where the responsive design part comes in. You can buy WordPress themes on hundreds of websites (and actually download many for free as well), and these themes are uploaded into your implementation of WordPress. Once uploaded you can choose to preview what your site will look like with the theme, and choose to then 'switch it on'. Most themes come with a number of customization options, including things like changing colours, menu options and types of page layouts. This means that when you preview the site, you won't normally see what it will finally look like, but it will give you some insights.

You need to make sure that you select a theme that is designed to be responsive and work on mobile devices. These responsive themes come with a number of mobile customization options, like allowing you to select what menu options will show on a mobile version of the site and what content should be visible. As such, these sites offer a good combination of true, responsive design and elements of building a mobile-specific version of your site, all working within one CMS.

There are lots of WordPress theme websites out there, and a Google search of the phrase 'WordPress theme' will give you a huge amount to look through and get a feel for the kind of things that are available. You can normally preview what your website could potentially look like and the theme websites also explain the customization options that will be available to you.

My favourite theme website is http://www.themeforest.net and it's actually where the theme for the website that accompanies this book was bought!

Figure 8.3 shows a wedding photography website built in WordPress using a downloadable responsive theme. Figure 8.4 illustrates the same website as seen on an iPhone, showing the mobile, one-column design, with menu navigation shown as a drop-down menu that launches a mobile selector. We'll discuss mobile design later in this chapter.

Step 3.1: Define your customization and get a freelancer to implement

At this stage you have two choices. Do you want to try and install WordPress, install your theme and then customize things, or do you want somebody to do all of this for you? If you don't really need any major customization and you think you can manage the skills in the box below, it's a great learning curve to do this yourself. If you need a fair bit of customization, don't want to bother with this type of thing or are nervous about your technical abilities, there is a quick and cost-effective alternative.

Figure 8.3 Website built in WordPress using downloadable responsive theme

Simply Wedding Photography
Affordable Wedding and Civil Partnership Photograpy

Home   Image Gallery   Weddings   Civil Partnerships   Prices   About me

Affordable Photography

Simply Wedding Photography offers affordable wedding and civil partnership photography that does not compromise on quality or style for couples getting married in Sussex.

My aim is to offer people the wedding photographs that they want at a price that they can afford.

Based in Brighton, I will travel to West Sussex and East Sussex and will consider other locations on request.

Prices overview

All the packages include a minimum of 150 High resolution photographs of your Wedding Day on a CD ROM - If more photographs are taken on the day you will also receive these.

Wedding Photos Price Package 1 £450.00
Ceremony and Reception (3hrs)

Wedding Photos Price Package 2 £600.00
Getting ready, Ceremony and Reception (5hrs)

Wedding Photos Price Package 3 £800.00
Getting ready, Ceremony, Reception and Meal (7hrs)

Testimonials

"Susana offers an excellent service which is outstanding value for money. She really did capture our wedding day just as we remember it."

"I wanted my day to be a relaxed as possible and Susana reflected this perfectly in her photographs."

"Thank you for the photo's. We love all of them and are busy showing them to everyone"

© 2013 Internet Internet   Simply Wedding Photography - 07748926452

SOURCE: www.simplyweddingphotography.co.uk

Figure 8.4 Website built in WordPress on an iPhone

SOURCE: www.simplyweddingphotography.co.uk

There are a number of websites that allow you to submit a brief for a project and allow freelancers or companies around the world to give you a quote and submit their services for the work. My favourite of these websites is http://www.upwork.com and it is where I have found the developers that I work with on a regular basis now.

The most important thing about using one of these freelance websites is to make sure you submit a thorough and well-thought-out 'brief', or in other words, a project specification. The more detailed, clear and unambiguous your specification, the more likely that the work delivered by the freelancer will be what you were hoping for and expecting. This specification may include things like: text describing functionality of your mobile site; screen shots indicating where you'd like changes; scanned sketches or diagrams communicating your ideas clearly.

Once you post your specification you then sit back and wait for developers to submit their quotes. When the quotes do start to come in, your next big problem is selecting which one to choose. Cost will obviously be a factor, but more importantly you need to judge the freelancers' abilities and understanding of your project specification. You'll also need to consider things like reliability, project management skills and communication skills. Bear in mind your freelancer might be on the other side of the planet, and that you may not share the same first language. I am based in the UK and work regularly with developers in Turkey and India via Elance.com with absolutely no problems.

A good way to select a freelancer is to look at their response and see if they seem to understand your specification clearly. You then normally look at their work experience and see how much work they have completed on the freelancer site you are using. You can normally see how many jobs they have completed, their overall total billings (so you can get a feel for the scale of projects they are working on) and what their feedback is like on previous projects.

Just like any online review, we need to know how to differentiate good, useful and honest reviews from those that have been placed falsely in order to try and persuade you into placing work with a particular freelancer. My experience has shown that the amount of fake reviews on sites like these is fairly low, but there are some signs to look out for. The most obviously suspicious sign is when there only a few reviews, all on very low-cost projects, that all appear to be in the same tone and use similar language. This can show that the freelancer in question has posted jobs, completed them him- or herself and then left their own reviews!

A great way to minimize the risk is to post a small, low-cost job first of all and try out a freelancer. If you find they are reliable and effective, you may then want to scale up to do more work with them. My experience using freelancers this way has been absolutely exceptional, and I am still amazed at what great work I can get done at such low cost. Although I can do lots of customization work myself, it is often easier and faster to get it done by a freelancer.

Step 3.2: Install WordPress and your theme

If you are feeling confident of your skills or you are keen to learn, setting up your own WordPress site and installing the theme yourself can be very straightforward. However, if you want to do customization beyond the basic functionality of WordPress (changing text and images, for example) and beyond what your theme offers as standard, you will need more in-depth technical skills.

WordPress actually offers a very clear step-by-step guide to installing the system and there are very active discussion forums where you scan previous issues and ask questions. Get started by reading this installation guide: https://codex.wordpress.org/Installing_WordPress.

Useful hands-on skills

If you want to be able to deploy a WordPress website yourself, you're going to need the following very simple skills. If you have no interest whatsoever in doing something like this yourself, it's still worth understanding some of the key steps involved.

Hosting control panels

Most hosting, and particularly hosting of the kind you'll need for WordPress, will generally come with a control panel. There are normally two levels of control panels: one for managing your hosting account and one for actually managing your web server. We are most interested in the web server control panel. This will allow you to do things like set up e-mail addresses and a database. There are common platforms for doing these kinds of things, and cPanel and Plesk are two of the most popular. They are generally very easy to use and fairly intuitive. Normally the most complicated thing you'll need to do is to create a database, which basically involves clicking on a 'database' icon, selecting something like 'create' and then giving it a name and password. Most often, the database element of your web hosting will use something called MySQL, and your web control panel is allowing you to interact with this in an easy way.

FTP software

In order to put files onto your web hosting space, you are going to need some file transfer protocol (FTP) software. There are plenty of different solutions out there for PC, Mac and even for mobile devices. Your hosting will come with an FTP username and password, and you'll need to put these into your software in order to navigate your web server and add/remove files.

HTML and PHP

You really don't need to know any PHP (a server-side scripting language) or HTML to install WordPress. However, I think it's increasingly important that more of us understood some of the technologies behind how the web works. I'm not suggesting that we should all go out and become developers, but a good knowledge of how the different technologies work and fit together can be massively useful. It will allow you to interact with developers more easily, mean you can understand what you are being told, and know how to ask the right kinds of questions. It also means you'll be much better at writing project specifications.

A great place to learn the fundamentals (and beyond) are the tutorials on html.net that can be found at: http://html.net/.

That's pretty much it. Combine these skills (and you can skip the HTML and PHP bit) with a download of WordPress and some hosting, and you'll be able to set up your own website. There are also some more great tutorials online and we've listed some of these on our website: http://www.targetinternet.com/mobilemarketing/.

A user-centred approach to mobile sites

Just like all web design, all mobile site design and planning should start by considering some key questions. What are our business objectives and how does our mobile approach tie in with this? What are the users' requirements and how can we help them achieve these requirements using a mobile site? Once we are sure that these two questions are answered and aligned we can then start to build our mobile site.

However, we always need to remember much of the design process is based on theory, planning and assumptions (no matter how well researched this work is). Therefore, we need to make sure we factor user testing and ongoing improvement into our mobile site development process. Let's work through some of the key stages, as illustrated in Figure 8.5.

Figure 8.5 Mobile design and development: key elements of user-centred approach

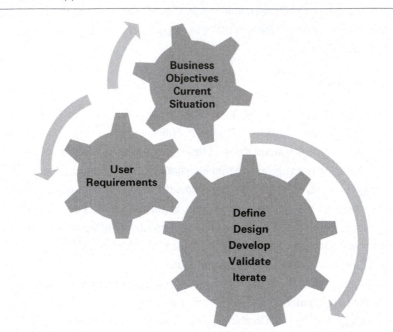

Current situation and business objectives

Although it may seem strange to suggest the first step of a *user*-centred approach is to think about business objectives, we need to frame the entire process. We need to consider how a mobile site aligns with our overarching business objectives and define the purpose for which it exists. It is very easy to create mobile sites, apps, use social media or carry out any digital activity for the sake of doing it, rather than the activity actually having a clear alignment with business objectives.

It may be that a mobile site is essential to help potential customers research our products and services effectively. It may be that the functionality we offer gives the user something useful that helps bolster our value proposition in the market. Whatever the business objectives, this should frame our plans and can help inform budgetary decisions and help us get internal buy-in where needed.

We should also at this stage benchmark our current situation and the environment we are working in. Some of the questions you need to answer are suggested below:

- How does a mobile site align with my business objectives?
- How much of our existing traffic is on mobile devices?
- What is the current mobile experience?
- How do we currently rank in the search engines for mobile search?
- What do our competitors offer via mobile sites?
- How do our competitors rank in the search engines for mobile search?
- What resources do we have, what can we commit and what will be the ongoing requirements?
- What skills do we have in-house and what partnerships do we have to achieve this project?

Once we have benchmarked our current situation we can move on to trying to understand the potential mobile site user. Always remember, though, this should be seen as an iterative process, and you may need to revisit this step a number of times as new questions and challenges arise.

User requirements

At this stage we get into the essential process of trying to understand the key user requirements. There is enough theory on this topic to fill the rest of the book very easily. Don't worry, we won't do that. We'll focus on the key issues, best practice, and point out some great resources on the topic.

User-centred design resources

As normal you can find more resources on our website: http://www.targetinternet.com/mobilemarketing/.

It's also worth checking out the site below as well. It's my favourite resource on all things about usability by the great company WebCredible (no commercial relationship!): http://www.webcredible.co.uk/user-friendly-resources/.

There are a number of theories on how best to understand user requirements, so I've highlighted some key options below. Essentially we are trying to understand the tasks mobile site users will be carrying out and what their end goals are. Once we understand this, we should be able to develop a mobile site that helps the user to carry out these tasks and achieve their goals in the most effective way possible.

Personas

Personas are fictional characters that try to encompass as many of the characteristics of the target audience as possible. Any set audience may encompass a number of different personas, and these personas can be created to varying levels of detail.

A basic persona may just include things like key needs, desires and motivators, whereas a very detailed persona may be given an elaborate background story including work details, family, personal values and demographics like age and location.

The aim of the persona is to give us something to test our mobile designs against and allow us to ask some key questions. Would the design we have suggested match the needs of this persona? How would the needs of different personas vary, and how does this impact our design?

The following is a very brief example persona. It describes an individual and highlights the key issues in their life that may impact what they want and need from any particular mobile site:

Example persona

Susana is a mid-thirties professional woman with two children and a very busy life. She is technically savvy and an early adopter of many technologies. She needs the technology she uses to be reliable and robust as it is used during work and family time. Her key motivators are lack of time, need to balance work and family life, as well a desire to be stylish and express her creative side.

So from this example we can start to make a number of assumptions about what will be important in our mobile site. The context of how this persona will impact our design will depend on our business objectives and the scenario we are working within.

Scenarios

Scenarios are imagined circumstances in which we place our personas, and map out the key circumstances, needs and activities that may occur. This means as well as using the persona to understand individual needs, the scenario gives us the context. This can include things like physical location at a particular time, a set of circumstances or events, as well as external factors such as time pressures.

Example scenario

Your persona is travelling to a business conference and needs to find out as much about your organization as possible while travelling and at the conference. The conference itself is only for a few hours and there is limited internet connectivity.

From this scenario we can see that ease of navigation (due to using a mobile device while travelling), prioritization of content (due to limited time) and a focus on fast download speeds (due to limited bandwidth) will all be important.

Use cases

A use case is a step-by-step description of the interaction between the persona and the mobile device/mobile site. This allows us to map how the device and mobile site will be interacted with, click by click. It also allows us to see the steps that are being taken by the persona and to understand how the flow of a particular task can be optimized.

Example use case

1 The user searches for the company name on their device in Google.

2 The Google search returns results with the company name.

3 The user clicks on the company search result.

4 The mobile version of the website is loaded.

5 The user then clicks on the menu to find the 'About Us' section of the site.

6 The About Us page loads.

7 The user scans the page to look for key information.

8 The user clicks on the 'Find Us at Conference X' logo.

9 A PDF document is downloaded showing stand location.

This use case serves a number of purposes. It gives us something with which to explore how the user will interact with the site and what the ideal steps are to achieve the user's objectives. It also allows us to consider the scenario in more detail and consider how this will impact the functionality and design that we must provide.

Once we have fully defined our user requirements we can then move on to the next stage of implementation. Bear in mind, though, that up until this stage, all of our planning, even if detailed and well thought out, is mostly based on assumptions.

Define, design, develop, validate, iterate

This stage of the process is all about testing our assumptions in the real world. We use the previous two stages (current situation and user requirements) to help us define what our mobile site should do, and how it should do it. We then look at the output from the user requirements stage in more detail and use this to design our mobile site.

The initial design should take the form of a prototype. A prototype is a version of the site that has not required full development but gives us enough to start testing our assumptions. We can then take this prototype and test it against the personas, scenarios and use cases we have developed. This will allow us to start to iterate our ideas and improve them according to all of the research and planning work we have already done.

We may also be able to use these prototypes (which may be just wire-frame sketches of what the site will look like and how pages are connected to one another) and test them in the real world. An interview process with some members of our potential audience can help us test and improve our ideas further.

At this stage, when we are happy we have refined and revised our plans as much as possible, we then commit to the development of our mobile site. We hold back on this stage until we are sure we have thoroughly tested our assumptions, because changing things after the development stage can become expensive, whereas changing at the prototyping stage is generally far lower cost.

Prototyping and wireframes

Wireframes are representations of what your site will be laid out like, showing the key elements of the page without any detailed design. These wireframes can be highly effective in mapping out ideas, before we get distracted by the graphical design elements of our sites. Clickable wireframes allow us to click through these wireframe diagrams and see how pages are connected to one another. This can allow for a basic form of user testing to see if navigation aligns with users' expectations.

My favourite wireframing tool is Balsamiq Mockups (see Figure 8.6). It's easy to use and allows you to create clickable wireframes very quickly: http://www.balsamiq.com/products/mockups.

Figure 8.6 Example wireframe in Balsamiq Mockups

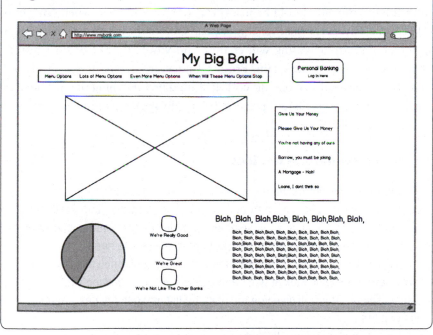

Only once we are happy with the layout and functionality, and we have tested our designs against our assumptions, should we start thinking about graphic design. When I say graphic design, I am referring to the visual identity graphical elements of our mobile sites. I say this because if we go out and ask a designer to mock up our site early on in the development process, it is very likely that we are going to get distracted by these designs. The reality is that a user-centred approach should consider functionality first; then graphic design when applied to this can enhance and improve it. However, the most beautiful site in the world will be useless if you don't get the functionality right.

I am certainly not dismissing graphic design as unimportant. I actually believe that the visual elements of a site can enhance the functionality massively when thought out correctly. We just shouldn't decide what something should look like before we know what it does.

The final stage after prototyping is development, when we actually start to build our sites. No site is ever completed, mobile or otherwise. The first iteration of your site should be just that, an iteration. Even when you get to what you believe is the final version of your site, soon enough the environment in which you are operating will change and you will need to start testing, changing and improving again. From a budgetary perspective I never look at web development as a one-off cost. It should be something that is budgeted for as an ongoing cost and a project that is always developing.

Testing on mobile devices

There is no true alternative for actually testing on each of the mobile devices you are expecting your audience to use. However, there are a number of great online services that can help you test your mobile sites out if you don't have access to the particular device you need.

A good place to start is to look at your existing web analytics (assuming you have some) and look at what mobile devices your existing site is being accessed on. This will give you an initial hit list of what devices you need to test first.

Google's Mobile-Friendly test will analyse your website from both a technical and usability point of view to analyse the suitability of your site for a wide range of mobile devices: https://www.google.co.uk/webmasters/tools/mobile-friendly/.

The Mobile Phone Emulator site offers a whole range of different devices that you can simulate, allowing you to see what your site will look like on various platforms. It also has settings so that it can display these in real-life size on your computer screen: http://www.mobilephoneemulator.com/.

The sooner you can get real users trying out your site the better (in controlled circumstances!). What I mean is that when you have a version of your site that is usable, even if it is unfinished and still has bugs, invite some users to try it out. Since there may be lots of problems still with the site, you may wish to do this on a one-to-one basis. My general experience is that even fairly basic usability testing, like asking a number of people to carry out the same task, will highlight key issues with your designs.

So you work towards a 'final' design, test, learn and improve on an ongoing basis. At some point you must decide to go 'live' and release your new mobile site into the world. Make sure that there are easy ways for users to feed back to you, so you can continue to improve things.

Ongoing maintenance

Once you achieve your beautifully planned and designed mobile site, you need to remember that you must commit to ongoing maintenance. With the world of mobile marketing moving so quickly, new devices, operating systems and changing user requirements are going to mean your site needs to change. If you don't adjust, what was a perfect site will in a short period of time become a business problem.

Mobile sites: conclusions

As you can see, there is a lot to consider when building mobile sites. You need to understand the technical aspects of mobile sites, but most importantly you must think about the reasoning behind the site in the first place. Poor use of technology can ruin an otherwise well-thought-out mobile site, but a site without a user-centred design approach is unlikely to stand a chance in the first place.

Mobile and e-mail

The majority of e-mails are now opened on a mobile device (Lewkowicz, May 2016). The reality, however, is somewhat more complicated. Many of us use our mobile devices to 'triage' our e-mails, that is, we use our mobile devices to monitor our incoming e-mail and respond to anything urgent. Non-urgent and more complex e-mail is generally responded to from a desktop or laptop in many cases (this is a reflection of the current limitations of mobile devices in many cases). This means we need to make sure our e-mails are fully optimized for the multi-screen journey.

Focusing on mobile users

In this chapter we'll look at each element of e-mail marketing in turn, but we need to keep mobile users at the heart of this journey. Bear in mind your ability to do this will be highly impacted by your e-mail service provider (ESP). For example, in Figure 9.1, you can see the options in MailChimp (a popular ESP that we will explore later in this chapter) for previewing your e-mails on various mobile devices.

E-mail isn't exciting

I don't agree with this statement one bit, and I'll explain why in a moment, but let's start with an example. If I run a webinar or a conference talk and I include the phrase 'latest trends in social media' I'm pretty sure I'll fill the room (virtual or otherwise). However, if we talk about some element of e-mail marketing, it just won't get the same level of response. Most of us are interested in what's new and what's changing, and many of the core principles of e-mail marketing have been the same for some time. The issue is that not many of us are following these principles and we'd rather try something new than improving what we're already doing.

Figure 9.1 Using an ESP to preview e-mail display on various e-mail clients

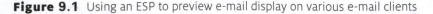
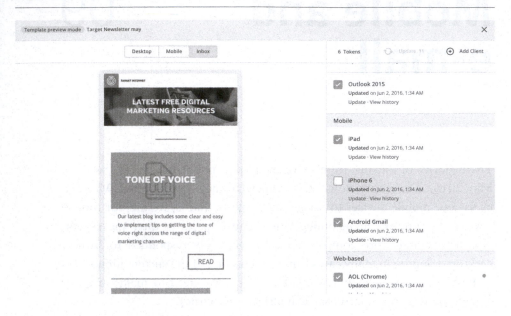

Ease of iteration

The single greatest thing about e-mail, in my opinion, is the ability to test, learn and change quickly and easily. Trying different versions of pages on your website or creating different apps can be expensive, time-consuming and often fraught with technical problems. Trying different e-mail subject lines, calls-to-action, length of copy are all extremely easy to test, assuming you are using the right ESP.

An ESP will allow you to store e-mail lists, create and send e-mail campaigns and track results for you. How well suited your ESP is to your needs will have a direct impact on how effective your e-mail campaigns can be. There are dozens of different ESPs out there, ranging from the basic, through to highly sophisticated systems that could be used as CRM systems in their own right. We'll explore what we need from an ESP in more detail in a moment, but first we need to look at the state of the e-mail market and dispel some myths.

The decline of spam and rise of bacn

You are probably very aware of the concept of spam, defined as unsolicited e-mail communications. As we have said, spam is actually on the decrease and a range of security and technology solutions are helping to progress this fight. What is generally on the rise, though, is bacn (pronounced 'bacon')! Bacn is defined as the range of e-mails that we have signed up for but don't see as relevant and never read. Over time we subscribe to more and more newsletters, we get service and social media updates we never read and are generally getting more e-mail that, although not truly spam, isn't relevant or useful to us.

Increasingly, web mail clients like Gmail are trying to separate this kind of e-mail from e-mails that are relevant by placing these e-mails under separate tabs. Different systems have different ways of judging the relevance of an e-mail, but very often it is based on user behaviour. If you regularly open and click on e-mail from a particular address, these systems will learn your behaviour and identify that an e-mail is relevant and they are more likely to place this e-mail in your main inbox. Therefore, getting engagement and clicks on every one of your e-mails becomes even more important as it will impact whether your future e-mails are seen as well.

There are also services like Unroll.me and Sanebox.com, that offer us services to help filter our e-mail, unsubscribe from unwanted newsletters and summarize lower priority content. All of this means that if our e-mails aren't seen to provide value, our target audiences just won't see them in the first place.

Focusing on relevance

This movement toward separating essential e-mails from promotional e-mails means that if we use e-mail as a broadcast channel, focusing sales messages, we are likely to get lower and lower response rates. The nature of mobile users trying to 'triage' their e-mail means we have precious few seconds to demonstrate the value of our content. We need to focus on using a range of techniques and technologies available to us to make our e-mail as tailored, relevant and useful as possible to our audience, and that's what we'll explore in this chapter.

This doesn't mean that you can't send promotional e-mails with products and special offers. If I ask you to send me special offers that's what you should do, but they need to be the right offers for me, sent at the right time, at the right level of frequency. And if I've signed up for a newsletter, don't just send me sales messages. The general approach I apply to e-mail marketing when not working on an e-commerce basis, and an immediate online sale is not the proposed outcome, is to consider the principles of content marketing. There should be a ratio of commercial to non-commercial content in your e-mails, and by that I mean really providing value through your e-mail content. Many of my clients work on an 80/20 rule, that is 80 per cent non-commercial, useful content, and 20 per cent about stuff they want to sell you. I'd suggest you go even further and aim for a 90/10 or 100 per cent non-commercial content. Providing useful content is the single best way to get your e-mail known and remembered, increase the likelihood of future e-mail opens and driving traffic to your site. Once you have the site visitor, you have the opportunity to build trust and awareness and potentially drive somebody along your sales funnel.

E-mail and the user journey

Once we understand the impact e-mail marketing has on our potential user journey and how effectively it can work as one of our digital touch points we can start to really look at the great return on investment (ROI) e-mail marketing can offer.

The importance of tracking code

When we look at our web analytics to try and understand where our web traffic is coming from and how it is impacting our bottom line, Traffic Sources is an essential report. In Google Analytics these are found under the Acquisition reports and are broken down into some key areas: organic search is traffic from sites like Google (but not paid advertising from these sites); referrals are visits from other websites; social are visits from social websites; and then we come to direct visits. Supposedly direct traffic is traffic that comes to your site when somebody types your web address directly into their browser or has bookmarked your site and visits by selecting that bookmark. What direct traffic actually represents is visits that your analytics package has no idea where they have come from.

This is a really important thing to understand in regard to e-mail, because unless we add tracking code (which we'll explain in a moment and cover in more detail in Chapter 19 on analytics) to the links in our e-mails, then people clicking on these links will show up as direct traffic and we won't be able to differentiate where they came from. So when we send out our e-mail campaigns, we'll see an increase in direct traffic, but can't 100 per cent identify that as being from our e-mail.

Tracking code basically involves adding some information to each of our links, so when a visitor arrives on our site we can use analytics to identify exactly where they have come from. You can see the Google URL builder that allows us to generate this code in Figure 9.2 and see Chapter 19 to learn more about tracking code. It is also possible that your ESP gives the option to automatically add tracking code, which can be a great time-saver.

Figure 9.2 Using Google URL builder to generate tracking code for an e-mail campaign

URL builder form

Step 1: Enter the URL of your website.

Website URL *

www.mywebsite.com/mypage

(e.g. http://www.urchin.com/download.html)

Step 2: Fill in the fields below. **Campaign Source, Campaign Medium and Campaign Name** should always be used.

Campaign Source *

Summer

(referrer: google, citysearch, newsletter4)

Campaign Medium *

email

(marketing medium: cpc, banner, email)

Campaign Term

(identify the paid keywords)

Campaign Content

Google and the Google logo are registered trademarks of Google Inc; used with permission

Going beyond last click

To understand how e-mail is having an impact on our overall marketing efforts, we need to understand where it fits into the user journey and how it is impacting the bottom line. We may expect somebody to read our e-mail, then directly buy our product or fill in our lead generation form. However, it's more likely that e-mail will be one of many touch points that build up our relationship over time. For this reason, we need to consider the analytics results from our e-mail campaigns carefully and make sure we are going beyond the last click. We explore this idea a lot more in Chapter 19 on analytics, but fundamentally we are understanding each step of the journey that leads somebody to carry out an action that we desire. For example, as we can see in Figure 9.3, there may be a number of different paths through to conversion. For example, as we can see at the top of Figure 9.3, I may get an e-mail, some time later do a search triggered by something I experienced in that e-mail, and then go on to carry out some form of online conversion. Alternatively, as we can see at the bottom of Figure 9.3, I might have just done a search and immediately converted. In both cases, if we looked at analytics from a last-click perspective, the source of the conversion would be seen as the search, as this was the last click before conversion. By that logic, we might challenge why we are even bothering with e-mail marketing and pull the plug on this activity. But if we do that, we won't get the search that followed and we won't get the conversion.

So in order to really get the most from analytics when we are thinking about e-mail marketing we need to have tracking code in place and make sure we are looking beyond the last click. Happily, Google Analytics provides some excellent reports to allow us to do this in the shape of Multi-Channel Funnels. We look at this report in more detail in Chapter 19, but essentially it allows us to see which channels a user of our site employed up to 90 days before they convert. That is, what are the different steps and channels that were chosen in any of the user journeys that ended with one of goals being completed.

Figure 9.3 Considering each step in the user journey and going beyond a last-click mentality

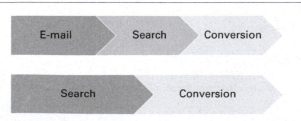

Selecting an e-mail service provider

To really get the most out of e-mail marketing we have said we need to focus on relevance. In order to do that we are going to need to think about segmenting our data, targeting the content, testing different elements of our campaigns and really making best use of the channel. In order to do that, and to make it easy to do, we need to select the right tool, and generally that will be some form of ESP. These tools typically work around three key areas: building, segmenting and targeting your e-mail list; building and sending your e-mails; and finally reporting on the results. Each of these areas can be extended to offer all sorts of functionality like scheduling, automatic triggering and social media integration, all of which we'll explore later.

The key thing is, you don't want to get stuck with a system that limits your capability but you also don't want to pay for things that you don't need. We've highlighted a few different ESPs in this chapter, but there are new entrants all the time and many are very similar. To help you choose, we've highlighted some of the key considerations below.

Enter the monkey

MailChimp is a very popular and low-cost ESP. It has a very intuitive interface, loads of advanced functionality and is one of the cheapest ESPs in the market. It is also fully geared up to help you build mobile-optimized campaigns. They charge by the size of your list, rather than by how many e-mails you send, which can be a real cost saver if you are sending a lot of e-mails.

So what are the downsides? First of all, all support is done online, meaning you don't have an account manager you can call on. Also, it's a self-service system, and although the interface is very straightforward, it's down to you (although there is nothing stopping you from bringing in a third party to assist you). You also need to pay using a credit/debit card, meaning if you can't pay this way, it's not for you. Also, if you need some form of customization or really advanced integration it may not be the right choice (although they do have an API that lets developers do all sorts of things with the system).

I love MailChimp. I use it for my business and I love the fact that it means I can test and learn quickly and easily. There are lots of other ESPs out there, but MailChimp is often a very good starting point. http://www.mailchimp.com.

Gaining opt-ins and building a list

In order to do any e-mail marketing we are going to need to collect an e-mail list, and the rules on how we can collect data change from country to country. It's also not just a matter of following the rules, but really about following best practice in order to ensure the quality of our lists and avoid annoying our target audience. Like many things in digital marketing, we tend to get distracted by volume when carrying out e-mail campaigns, and the question often asked after each campaign is 'How many e-mails have we sent?' and 'How many people are on our lists?'. What we should really be focusing on is the quality of our lists and the actual results our campaigns get. We actively don't want people on our list who don't want our e-mails, otherwise we are just creating a negative touch point that will damage our brand image. I'm sure you can think of at least one company that keeps e-mailing you with irrelevant or overly sales-based content, and over time it creates a negative impression of that brand.

Best practice in regard to opt-in is to follow a 'double opt-in' approach: allow people to fill in a sign-up form (more on that in a moment) and then send them an e-mail that they need to click on to confirm their opt-in. This might sound like a slightly laborious process but most ESPs will fully automate this process for you. Also, the fact the user has filled in a form and bothered to click on a link achieves two things: first, they have self-qualified by showing they are actively interested in what you have offered based on the fact they have actually made some effort to sign up; secondly, this sign-up process gives you actual evidence they have signed up, otherwise anybody could take your e-mail address and sign you up for any e-mail list!

Sign-up forms

Rather than trying to collect huge amounts of data at the point of sign-up, which will be a barrier to getting opt-ins, I generally recommend you keep the amount of information you ask for initially to a minimum. You then have the opportunity to prove the value of your e-mails and then ask for more information by using surveys, questionnaires or polls on an ongoing basis. You also need to consider the types of data you may want to collect, whether you really will use that data and whether your ESP is capable of storing it and using it. We may also want to think about how we are going to move this data between our ESP and our CRM.

Mobile and sign-up forms

One of the greatest and ongoing frustrations for mobile users is pop-over e-mail sign-up forms. For example, you visit a website and are reading a great blog post. After a few seconds a pop-over form covers the page and asks you to sign up to the website's e-mail list. This is no problem on a laptop, you simply click the close window button on the top right corner of the pop-over. Unfortunately, many of these pop-overs are not built with mobile users in mind, and the close button is unreachable on a mobile device, leaving the user stranded on a useless page. If you are going to use pop-over forms, it is essential to thoroughly test them on mobile devices.

The two key things that concern people when they are signing up to an e-mail list are: what are you going to do with their data, and how often are you going to e-mail them? Ideally at this stage you will clarify both points with a statement along the lines of 'We will never pass on your details to anybody else and we won't e-mail you more than once a week'. You can also have a link through to your privacy policy that outlines clearly what you do with data, but in my experience very few people actually read these.

List segmentation

As you build an e-mail list, you need to consider what differentiates the individuals on your list and what kinds of different content may be relevant to each of these segments. It's essential that your ESP allows you to collect data and add fields of information to your list in a way that will be practically useful for segmenting your lists in the future.

For example, you may want to send different e-mails to people living in different geographical locations and you'll therefore need to collect and store that data. It could be that you want to store this data separately in your CRM system, but for now let's assume we are adding more information to our ESP list.

Different ESPs have different approaches and limitations to this, but increasingly many ESPs allow you to add a huge number of additional fields (in some cases an unlimited number) that you can then use to segment and personalize your e-mail.

The benefits and risks of personalization

Personalization in e-mails generally often refers to the process of inserting personalized content such as your name, job role, company name or location into an e-mail. It can also refer to the process of segmentation or dynamically building content, but we'll explore these concepts later.

So if we are talking about inserting your name into an e-mail to personalize it, what actual impact does that have? Different studies show different results, and it certainly has to be seen in the context of your overall e-mail efforts, but there is generally a small increase in click-through rate (CTR). However, if you get the data wrong and insert the wrong job title or name, the damage will far outweigh any good you would have done. Therefore, only do this form of personalization if you trust the quality of your data 100 per cent.

We can segment our lists in a number of different ways but we are generally talking about segmenting our lists based on collected data and by preference. That basically means that we have collected some information from an individual on our list and then used this to personalize their e-mail. This may be in the form of sending particular content, sending a particular format of e-mail or sending at a particular time or frequency, all based on what data you have collected.

This approach can be very effective in making e-mails more relevant and improving open rates and CTR. In fact, improvements of around 15 per cent in open rates and up to 63 per cent in CTR are entirely possible when taking this approach (MailChimp, 2016).

Open rates and click-through rates

Two of the most commonly discussed statistics we get from our e-mail campaigns are open rates and click-through rates. It's worth understanding these in a bit more detail so we understand where they are useful and what their limitations are.

Open rate tries to tell you how many people have actually opened your e-mail. I say tried, because unfortunately, the way this is calculated is inherently inaccurate. An e-mail is registered as open when an image in that e-mail has been loaded. So, you bring an e-mail up in your e-mail client, one of the images loads and that tells the ESP that the e-mail must have been opened. This image is generally a single pixel image hidden at the bottom of your e-mail, often referred to as a web beacon.

There are two problems with this approach. The first is that even if you open an e-mail for half a second and then delete it, as long as the image loads, the e-mail will show as being opened. Now although this is technically true, the open rate doesn't really paint a true picture of what happened for us. The other problem with relying on images being loaded to indicate that an e-mail has been opened means that when an e-mail is viewed on an e-mail client that doesn't load the images, you won't know it has been opened. It has been suggested that around 50 per cent of users don't see images automatically, which could mean some fairly unreliable data being reported as open rates.

This doesn't mean we should abandon looking at open rates, however. In fact, we are still using them as a benchmark, as at least we are comparing like for like from one campaign to the next or within split testing (which we'll talk about more in a moment). We just can't rely on them as an entirely accurate representation of how many people open our e-mails.

Click-through rate (CTR) is the other key measure we to tend to look at, and although a far more accurate measure, we can rely on it too much. Obviously, getting a click on your e-mail and driving a visit through to your website is great; however, that is just part of the journey. It is entirely possible that everybody who clicks gets through to your website, takes one look, doesn't like the look of it and leaves immediately. You could therefore have a campaign with a 100 per cent CTR that was a complete failure!

So CTR is a useful measure but we then need to look at the visitors' behaviour on our site to really understand the true impact of our e-mail campaigns. So for true commercial insights we will need e-mail reporting, web analytics, and for goals to be set up in analytics. We'll also need to understand how these goals impact our business outcomes (and that's what Part Three of this book is all about).

This does highlight one of the potential weaknesses of e-mail marketing, however: even if you have the best e-mail campaign in the world, if your website doesn't match that standard, your campaign won't be as effective as it could be.

E-mail templates and design

We could fill an entire book with the discussions about e-mail design best practice, what works and what doesn't. The reason for this level of discussion is that the effectiveness of the design will depend on your target audience, the e-mail client, the device the e-mail is being read on, and a host of other factors. What that means is that we need to test for our particular list, and in fact we may find that different designs are more or less suitable for different lists and even segments of our lists. We'll explore all the different things you can test for your particular list in the testing section of this chapter (see page 98), but we highlight here the key principles that every e-mail should take into account.

Minimum font size

Apple recommends 17–22 pixels (px) and Google recommends 18–22 px for mobile devices, so go for 18px minimum.

Header images above the fold

Don't place large header images at the top of e-mails. They push your content further down the page, and when images are switched off your audience won't see anything apart from a missing image.

Blocked images display

Consider what your e-mail will look like when images are switched off. Make sure you have a 'click to view online' link (most ESPs will add these automatically). Also make sure all of your images have ALT text as this will display in many e-mail clients when images are switched off in place of the image.

Call-to-action placement and size

Consider where on the page your call-to-action will appear in various e-mail clients and try and keep it visible above the fold (before a user needs to scroll down to see the content). Bear in mind that the bottom right, where many calls-to-action end up, may not be the most suitable place and you may need multiple calls-to-action.

For call-to-action buttons Apple recommends 44px squared and Google recommends 48px squared for mobile users, so go for the higher of the two, 48px.

Scanability

Users try to assess the relevance of an e-mail as soon as they open it and decide if it is worth reading properly or not. Make sure your e-mail is scanable and that the key message comes across clearly and easily. Avoid large blocks of text, complicated layouts and poorly defined calls-to-action. Don't have multiple links close together.

Unsubscribe

Every e-mail should have an unsubscribe link in the footer and this will generally be automatically inserted by your ESP.

Footer

The footer of your e-mail should also include your physical postal address if you wish to be compliant with US e-mail regulations (CAN-SPAM).

Responsive e-mail design

Responsively designed e-mails attempt to adapt the e-mail according to the device it is displaying on and the screen's display size. This means that an e-mail will display differently on a smartphone, a tablet and a laptop screen. However, just as there are limitations in what we can do with e-mail design vs web design, there are limitations on the effectiveness of responsive e-mail design.

This limitation is because most responsive design principles rely on the support of media queries, a technique used to understand the size of a screen, and then adapt things accordingly. Unfortunately, media queries aren't supported by all e-mail apps. At the time of writing the most noticeable of these are the Gmail apps for iPhone and Android phones (however, Google have announced that Gmail will start supporting media queries very soon).

For a great summary of which apps do and don't support media queries take a look at the great guide on the Litmus website: https://litmus.com/help/e-mail-clients/media-query-support/.

E-mail templates

You have a few options to consider when creating e-mails and the templates that you use. You can design your own templates from scratch, edit an existing template from your ESP or use a template from another source. Each of your e-mails could be different, but in terms of brand consistency it makes sense to modify a particular template for a particular style of e-mail each time you send one. So for example you may have a newsletter template, an e-commerce template, etc.

Most ESPs will provide a set of standard e-mail templates that you can modify for your own use and many also provide a visual editor that lets you edit these templates without any coding skills. Alternatively, you may need to edit your template code yourself and upload the HTML. You could do this editing yourself if you have the skills or use a designer/developer to do this for you. There are lots of ESPs that offer these kind of services at an additional cost or you could use a freelancer website like UpWork.com. Always remember, though: e-mail template design is a very specific skill, and just because somebody can design a website doesn't mean they know all the peculiarities of design for the wide range of e-mail clients.

The most important thing to do with your e-mail template is make sure it displays properly on different e-mail clients and devices, and to do this you have two options, one easy and one hard! The hard option is to manually test your e-mail template on every possible different e-mail client and possible device combination. This very quickly becomes an impractical task because of the number of possible options. This is why inbox inspectors were created, in order to simulate what your e-mail will look like on each of these different display possibilities. Many ESPs have these built in, but if your system doesn't you can use a system like Litmus, shown in Figure 9.4.

Spam checking

We've already discussed the improvements in technology that are leading to the increased detection of spam e-mails. Unfortunately, the side effect of this is that your e-mail could be mistaken for spam by the many spam filters in operation and never reach its intended destination. In order to minimize the chances of this happening you can use a spam filter testing tool. This will try and gauge the likelihood of your e-mail ending up in a spam filter and will point out the key things you may want to change in your e-mail.

Your ESP should have one of these tools built in, but if it doesn't, Litmus.com also offers this service.

Figure 9.4 Previewing your e-mail's appearance on a wide range of clients and devices using Litmus.com

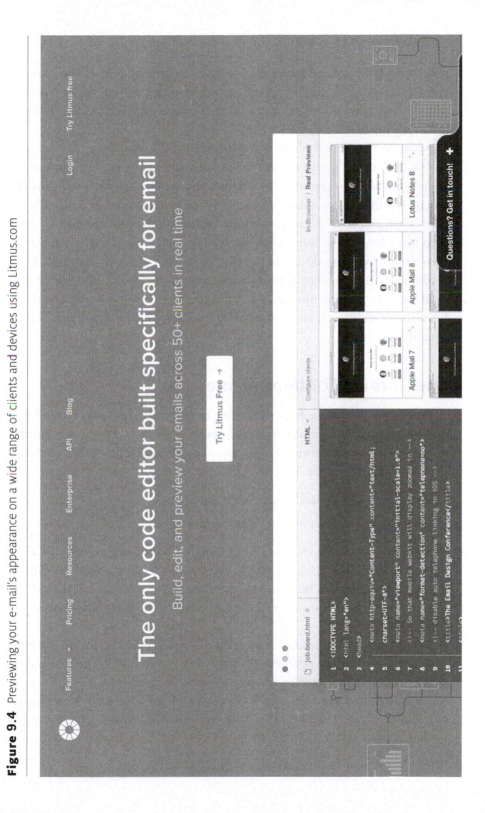

Sending and testing

Once you have created your great e-mail content and built the perfect targeted list, you are going to want to start sending your e-mails. There are quite a few things to consider at this stage and a range of testing options available to you.

Many ESPs will now allow you to carry out A/B split testing very easily, or you can manually split up your list in order to do this. The basic principle is that you take two segments of your lists and send each a variation of your e-mail, testing a particular feature of the e-mail (this could be subject line, copy length, etc – we highlight these different variables in a moment). You then learn from these tests, work out which one got the better results and then apply this learning to the remainder of your list. For example, you could take two segments of your list, each consisting of 15 per cent of the total list and run a test (making up 30 per cent of your list overall). You then learn from this list and send out the better variation to the remaining 70 per cent of your list.

Open rate or click-through rate

When carrying out these tests, depending on what element of our e-mail we are testing, we will need to look to the open rate or the CTR for our results to judge which were most the most successful. We can split which of these two measures we need to look at as follows:

- **Open rate:** subject line, time sent, 'from' address.
- **CTR:** all variations within the e-mail content.

Once we decide which element of our e-mail we are going to test, we also need to decide how long we are going to wait after sending the initial two tests until we can judge which were the more successful and send to the rest of our list. You can see how easy some ESPs make this process in Figure 9.5.

Something you do need to consider, however, is how the period of time you wait after sending your initial e-mails before sending to the remainder of your lists will impact your results. If you send out the test segments on a Tuesday and then send out to the remainder of your list on a Wednesday, you will potentially skew your results, because people react differently to e-mails on different days of the week.

Figure 9.5 The easy-to-use interface for sending A/B split-test campaigns using MailChimp.com

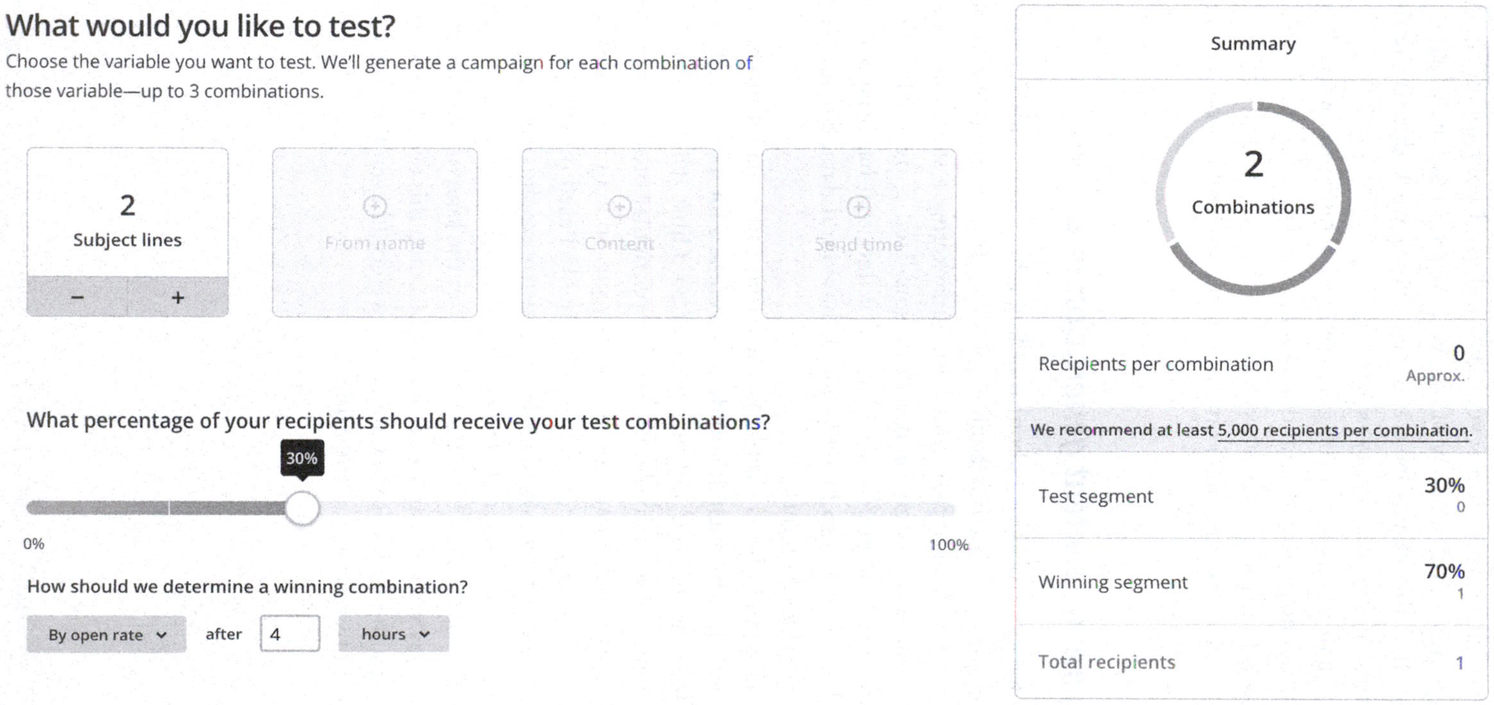

What would you like to test?

Choose the variable you want to test. We'll generate a campaign for each combination of those variable—up to 3 combinations.

2
Subject lines

−   +

From name

Content

Send time

What percentage of your recipients should receive your test combinations?

0%

30%

100%

How should we determine a winning combination?

By open rate ⌄   after   4   hours ⌄

Summary

2
Combinations

Recipients per combination   0
                                    Approx.

We recommend at least 5,000 recipients per combination.

Test segment   30%
                      0

Winning segment   70%
                      1

Total recipients   1

You could wait a clear seven days and send your follow-up e-mail at the same time of day and day of the week as your test e-mail, but even then you may find that things have changed over a week due to the time-sensitive nature of your news story or similar.

There is actually no 100 per cent ideal solution to this problem, but what you should do is understand which days of the week work best for you and how different days of the week compare. You can then choose to send your test and follow-up e-mail on days of the week when your audience reacts in similar ways.

Dynamic content generation and rules

So far we have talked about building a list, potentially segmenting this list and then sending out content, with various testing opportunities. Many ESPs allow you to take your e-mail marketing a stage further and generate even more well-segmented and personalized e-mails. They do this by not only looking at preference data, that is data that has been collected from the individual, but also by collecting behavioural data, dynamically generating e-mails based on this.

This could be as simple as triggering one e-mail a month since the last e-mail click-through. It could, however, be a lot more complex: look at user behaviour on your website in order to adjust what content is sent out in an e-mail. If an individual looks at a particular product, why not send them an e-mail about that product? If they put an item in their basket and didn't buy it, why not send a follow-up e-mail? Based on what they have clicked on in the last five e-mails, why not customize the content in the next e-mail based on these interested? Different ESPs allow you to do different things, so it's worth considering from the outset the kind of dynamic personalization you may want to carry out. Some ESPs take this even further by thoroughly integrating with CRM systems and we could even then start to look at the topic of marketing automation.

Message banks and business logic

An increasingly common approach to solving the problem of sending too many e-mails on different topics to the same individual is to use a message bank system. The basic concept is that we send a single e-mail that contains a number of different stories or pieces of content, but these pieces are selected and prioritized dynamically for a particular individual, based on a set of rules we define.

The rules we define can be simple or complex, but they dynamically select content and lace into a particular order from a 'bank' of messages (hence the name). This is only possible in some ESPs and there are some key challenges to consider. If the rules are too complex, we may need too many pieces of content in the bank to meet all of the requirements we have set. It is also possible that some parts of our list never receive a particular type of content because other pieces are always prioritized over it. The key here is to build your rules carefully, not get too complicated and test all of the possible outcomes.

E-mail marketing: conclusions

E-mail marketing is a hugely flexible area of digital marketing that can form an extremely effective part of our mobile marketing. It is also something that can be done badly very easily, so a suitable level of planning and resourcing is essential to get it right. Selecting the right ESP will impact everything you do in your e-mail marketing efforts, so select carefully and then make sure you are making full use of the various targeting and testing opportunities for mobile users.

How to build an app

10

At the time of writing, the Apple App Store has just passed 130 billion downloads and Apple has paid over US$50 billion dollars to app developers (Perez, 2016). This app 'gold rush', as it has been described, has led to a flurry of activity in the world of app development and the production of millions of apps. We'll look at the practicalities of building an app in this chapter, but first we are going to answer some essential questions and take a look at the app environment.

Many organizations rushed out and built apps just because they could. I witnessed dozens of conversations that started with the words 'We need an app' and ended in protracted discussion about what it could do, and how much it would cost. Just as we've discussed in the social media section of this book, though: just because you can do something doesn't mean that you should.

Mobile sites first

If you don't have a mobile-optimized website, forget about getting an app built and get your site fixed first. We've already talked about the huge increase in traffic to sites on mobile devices, and the reality is that this is actually more likely to be a user's initial experience of your mobile presence than an app. It's not that apps aren't also important, and in fact some studies have found that 35 per cent of users prefer the experience of apps to mobile sites (Quixey, 2015), but in reality if you actually need an app, you most likely also need a mobile-optimized site.

Bolstering value proposition

Just like any marketing activity we need to start by aligning our business objectives with user requirements and decide how our app can help achieve this. One thing for which apps can be fantastic is bolstering value proposition by delivering some form of online utility or entertainment.

Nike Training Club bolsters value proposition

One of my favourite examples of using an app to bolster value proposition is the Nike Training Club (NTC) app. It's very much in line with a clear value proposition of helping you achieve your athletic goals (rather than just being a company that makes sports clothes) and offers a range of features that are both practical, nicely designed and well thought out. The app is centrally focused around positioning Nike as experts that help assist an individual with their particular fitness needs.

Beyond this core functionality, NTC does a few things that show how appropriate use of the technology can be highly effective in tying together business objectives and user requirements. The rewards programme adds a level of gamification that encourages users to achieve training goals and then share these achievements. Users are rewarded for this activity and this drives social sharing and builds visibility of the brand. However, most important in my view is the data collection opportunity this gives Nike. By understanding their target audience's training objectives, challenges and the practicalities of how they implement these plans, Nike gains valuable insights.

The production and distribution of the app represent a sizeable investment, but when you compare this to the cost of running TV campaigns to build affinity and awareness, apps like this start to make a lot of financial success for a large brand like Nike. Also, bear in mind that the ongoing use of an app offers repeat brand exposure and can build affinity if the user requirements are met effectively.

Before we look at the specifics of developing apps, and address things like 'native' apps vs 'web' apps, let's consider the entire process and cover the common steps that you'll go through whenever you are developing an app.

The app-building process

We've repeated this mantra time and time again in this book, but let's start with some clear objectives. Why are you actually building an app in the first place? Is it all about bolstering your value proposition, as we've already discussed? Perhaps you are looking to build extra income so you can leave your job and live a life of travel and break the 9-to-5 routine (it's possible, but rare!)? Maybe you want to use an app to help sell your product, or maybe you're just doing it to see if you can? Whatever the answer, you need to have very clear expectations about what help you are going to need and what you can expect in terms of costs and revenues.

What is the 'post-app era'?

If you haven't read anything that was written by Gartner in their future predictions for 2020, you may be slightly confused or concerned by the idea of a post-app era, particularly if you are just creating your first app! Let's put things in context. What we are really talking about is that apps increasingly offer functionality that we aren't necessarily using within the app itself. Now that apps can run in the background when we are doing other things, they can increasingly offer services that react to factors like our location. The quote from Gartner that 'by 2020, smart agents will facilitate 40 per cent of mobile interactions, and the post-app era will begin to dominate' really refers to the growth of this ability (Gartner, 2015). It's less the fact that apps will die, but more that they will become less visible.

Understanding the skills involved

You may have a fantastic idea for an app that you are convinced will help you achieve your objectives, but you need to start laying down the path that will lead that app into the real world. I've listed some of the core stages below that you'll need to consider:

- app idea and initial concepts;
- app specification and wireframing;
- user interface design;

- visual design;
- technical development;
- testing;
- app store submission;
- app marketing;
- app maintenance;
- customer support.

Hopefully, you can see from this list that there is a lot more to the process than just coming up with an idea. In fact, many excellent apps fail because of a lack of ongoing marketing plans or because of poor maintenance and customer support.

Because of this list of different skills involved, it generally means that you are going to need some support with creating your app from multiple sources. We'll take a look at each of these steps and examine some of the things you'll need to consider.

Specification and wireframing

Just as with the construction of mobile sites, it is almost certainly worth spending as much time as possible on this initial stage. If you get this part right, you'll save yourself a lot of time and pain later on. A highly detailed and clear specification will lay out exactly what you are trying to achieve and how it should work. It will also consider fundamental elements of the interface design, like highlighting how pages are connected to one another, the flow through the app and so on. This basic graphical process is known as 'wireframing' and it helps to communicate your expectations of how the user will 'flow' through the app and the experience they will have. These wireframes will then be developed further when looking at user interface design and visual design, but this initial process will very much shape how the project develops. My favourite wireframing tool is Balsamiq Mockups. It's easy to use and allows you to create clickable wireframes very quickly: http://www.balsamiq.com/products/mockups.

As we are working through this specification process, there are a number of techniques we can use that will help make our initial plan as robust as possible and likely to succeed. We've already discussed these in depth in Chapter 8 on mobile sites, so it's worth taking a look at these if you haven't already, but I've summarized them below for quick reference.

Personas

Personas are fictional characters that try to encompass as many of the characteristics of the target audience as possible. Any set audience may encompass a number of different personas, and these personas can be created to varying levels of detail.

A basic persona may just include things like key needs, desires and motivators, whereas a very detailed persona may be given an elaborate background story including work details, family, personal values and demographics like age and location.

The aim of the persona is to give us something to test our mobile designs against and allows us to ask some key questions. Would the design we have suggested match the needs of this persona? How would the needs of different personas differ, and how does this impact our design?

Technical specification

You will also need to start considering technical aspects of your project at this stage as well. On which devices is it planned to work and what versions of these devices (iPhone 6 or 7, what about older versions, etc)? How quickly should the app respond to user input? What versions of the operating system will it work on?

There are many questions at this stage that will lead to important decisions down the line, and many people with great ideas for apps don't know how to answer these questions so leave them unasked. This then means that the app developer will decide how these questions are answered, and this may not be in line with what you have planned. For this reason, it is worth bringing a developer or someone with technical knowledge to help you define this stage of the project. Many see this early technical help as an unnecessary cost, but in my experience it can help you answer many questions early in the project before it gets expensive to change your mind.

Scenarios

Scenarios are imagined circumstances in which to place our personas and map out the key circumstances, needs and activities that may occur. This means that, as well as using the persona to understand individual needs, the scenario gives us the context. This can include things like physical location at a particular time, a set of circumstances or events, as well as external factors such as time pressures.

Use cases

A use case is a step-by-step description of the interaction between the persona and the mobile device/mobile site. This allows us to map how the device and mobile site will be interacted with, click by click. It also allows us to see the steps that are being taken by the persona and to understand how the flow of a particular task can be optimized.

By carrying out a robust specification process we will have made good progress in designing the information architecture (how the content fits together) and started to define the interaction design. We now need to define this interaction phase further and think about the other visual elements of the app.

Interaction and visual design

Once we have a clear view of the functionality and the fundamentals of our app we can start to consider the user interface in more detail and then consider the visual design. As we have discussed in Chapter 9, it is essential not to get too concerned with visual design too early in the project lifecycle. Although the visual elements of an app can be essential to its success, we need to get the core functionality right first. It is much easier to change visual design on top of a functional platform than it is to go back and fix the functionality.

I have divided the design phase into 'user interaction' design and 'visual' design for a number of reasons. First, I consider these to be very distinct parts of the app. Although they must work effectively together, by focusing on the importance of the interaction design, we can achieve a more usable app. In an ideal world the app should need no instructions for use, as its interface should be so intuitive that the user should immediately understand its functionality and interface. This ease of interaction is the job of the interaction designer.

The visual design is the visual identity or 'skin' of the app. You may find a designer with expertise in both interaction and visual design. You may even feel that your app only requires an interaction designer, as functionality is key.

Technical development and testing

At this stage you have a well-thought-out app, with key functionality, interaction design and visual identity defined. You are now ready to hand your idea over to a developer. The better defined your idea is, the more likely it is that you will get the app that you have visualized. You must also remember at this stage that you may need to make changes and modifications to your original design based on what the developer thinks is possible and/or appropriate. This is why it pays to get a developer involved in the specification in the first place. It is also advisable to use a designer with experience in mobile app design on the particular operating system(s) that you are planning on developing for.

We'll discuss in more detail the various operating systems and options you have when planning your app later, but your developer will clearly need skills in the particular approach you are taking. Also remember that many developers will be skilled in one approach but not necessarily the others, and if you are designing for multiple operating systems, you may need to use multiple developers.

You're going to need a developer to help you with testing, because until your app is in one of the app stores, you won't be able to get it into your phone without some technical assistance. There are a number of simulators that allow you to have a simulated device on your desktop, but these are never 100 per cent accurate and nothing beats real-world testing. Ideally, you need to test your app on as many devices and operating system versions as possible. In reality there are plenty of professional testers that can help with this process. You can use a freelancer or this may be a service that an agency offers as part of its overall service. We'll talk about freelancers and agencies more later.

The main reason for focusing your efforts on testing is that you need to meet certain criteria in order to be allowed to upload your app into the major app stores in the first place. Secondly, if you release an app with bugs and faults, you will upset the initial users, most likely get bad reviews and then get no more downloads. Invest the time to get it right the first time around.

App store submission

Submitting your app to the major app stores requires you to set up an account, agree that you have met the submission requirements and then to submit the appropriate file formats. This generally takes some technical knowledge so your first reaction may be to get your developer to do this for you. That approach is fine, but you need to make sure the account under which it is submitted belongs to you. This means you own the app and any profits it may make. It also means that you have control of the app for future changes. No problem having someone do this for you: but make sure everyone is clear on ownership and revenue.

The Apple App Store has a review process that can take some time. Most apps are reviewed within a number of days (Apple aim to complete the process for 90 per cent of apps within 48 hours), but the process can take months if you are rejected for some reason and have to resubmit multiple times. This means you will need to have a clear view on final launch date and take into account review times after submission. The process on Google Play (Google's app store) is generally more straightforward, but you still need to make sure you are meeting their submission guidelines.

App marketing

It is very easy to create a fantastic app that gets hardly any downloads. For every success story, there are tens of thousands of apps that never get anywhere. The pure volume of apps means that you need to get visibility to stand a chance of achieving success. The more downloads your app gets, the more visibility it tends to get in the app stores, and in turn the more downloads you get. It's a virtuous circle once it gets going, but it's hard to get going in the first place.

App store algorithms

The visibility you get in the app stores is based on a number of factors, and these factors or rules make up the algorithms behind the charts. There is a fair bit of complexity to these algorithms, but the core factors below decide whether you are at the top of the app charts and getting lots of visibility, or are nowhere to be seen:

- number of downloads;
- recency of these downloads;
- number of reviews;
- average star rating of reviews.

Based on this you want lots of downloads and positive reviews, concentrated over a period of time to get a boost up the charts. Clearly a well-thought-out marketing plan can help with this (as well as having a great app).

Outside the app stores

Due to the huge volumes of apps being published it is often hard to stand out within the app stores. For this reason, we need to make sure we are leveraging our other channels to drive app downloads. This can include promotion via social media sites (which we'll explore more in later chapters) as well as creating app landing pages. These landing pages can form part of our website and can drive increased downloads via cross-promotion and discovery via search engines. A novel use of SMS messaging is to use a website landing page to offer the service of sending an SMS to a mobile device in order to make the app download easy. We'll look at this option more in Chapter 18 on SMS.

Social media sharing and interaction

Make sure that you make it as easy and as likely as possible that a user will share your app via social media. Social sharing options within apps can work well, particularly when the user is rewarded in some way for sharing. This reward could be by highlighting an achievement within an app, or by giving extra rewards in exchange for sharing.

Gamification

Gamification is the principle of encouraging behaviours by rewarding a user in some way. This may be as simple as posting a high score to a public leader board (and remember this doesn't need to be limited to games; it could be for the most technical questions answered, etc). It can take more complex forms, such as being the first user to discover a piece of hidden content, or unlocking hidden features when certain activities are carried out.

The key thing that makes gamification work is that the reward should be valuable to the user. This may be in the form of content or reward, and very often that reward can just be recognition.

For my favourite example of gamification, take a look at the video for Jay-Z's *Decoded* book launch: http://www.youtube.com/watch?v= XNic4wf8AYg.

Another social media consideration is where you will interact and get feedback from your app users. The app stores can allow this in a limited way, but social platforms allow you to get more detailed feedback and to build engagement and advocacy with your audience.

App maintenance

Once your app is fully tested and live in the app store(s), you may think that your development requirements are fulfilled. In fact, there are two key reasons why you are going to need to keep on developing your app.

The first is user feedback. If you want to grow your downloads you need to keep improving things, reacting to user feedback and creating a better app. This will give you the opportunity to engage with your audience as well as differentiate yourself from the competition. Changes and updates give you something to talk about and can drive interest in your app. This also indicates to potential downloaders that your app is well maintained and can encourage more downloads. There are also a whole host of app developers who take existing ideas, improve them and then release these apps into the market. In order to stay ahead of this approach, you need to keep developing and refining your ideas.

Another reason that you will need to consider maintenance is the release of new phones and operating systems. As a new version of a phone, new device or new operating system is released, you are going to need to make sure your app is working properly. A bug caused by a new operating system or device can lead to bad reviews, and this can kill a previously successful app.

Customer support

Just as with any product or service, you need to look after your customers. Even for free apps, it's essential to react to feedback and fix bugs. This will help you reduce poor feedback and get the positive reviews that will encourage downloads and move you up the app charts.

Freelancers vs agencies

If you don't have the skills personally or inside your organization to create your app, you're going to need to find the skills elsewhere. You're going to need to understand the different options available to you in bringing in those necessary skills. First of all, here are the main differences between working with an agency and a freelancer.

Freelancers

Freelancers are generally the cheapest option (although some very experienced high-quality freelancers may be the same price as an agency). With a freelancer you are dealing with an individual – this in itself can have pros and cons. You are talking directly to the person doing the work so there is no incorrect channelling of communications or messages getting lost between people. It also means that if your freelancer is on holiday, off sick, or down the pub, there is nobody to speak to. They also generally won't have a finance or admin team and they probably won't have an office. This means meetings will happen at your premises or in a public place such as a cafe. This is a nice idea in theory but being surrounded by other people when you are discussing your top secret plan for launching the next Facebook or Twitter isn't ideal (although the coffee is often good). It's also unlikely you'll be their only client, so you need assurances in regard to how much of their time you are getting and their availability for discussing and feeding back on a particular project. All this aside, working with a freelancer can be very cost effective, and if you pick your freelancer well, the work can be excellent.

Agencies

Agencies will tend to have better facilities, including a range of staff for different tasks. This means there will generally be somebody to speak to when you need to – but don't make any assumptions about this and make sure you get a service level agreement (SLA) that guarantees availability, turnaround time, etc. One of the great joys of working with an agency (or pitfalls when it's not working properly) is your account manager. An account manager will be your first point of contact within a medium- to large-size agency (many agencies don't have account managers, particularly the smaller ones) and is generally responsible for channelling your requests to the right member of the team, getting feedback and reports for you, and generally fighting your side within the agency. This is great if you have a good account manager with whom you get on well. If you don't, it's a recipe for disaster as your main point of contact and communications channel will essentially be broken. Make sure you meet your account manager before signing a contract, and ask to speak to another client that has worked with the agency and has used the same account manager.

Agencies can be anything from a couple of freelancers working together to multinational companies with dozens of offices worldwide and teams of staff in the hundreds/thousands. Correspondingly, they can offer very different levels of service.

Questions to ask

The following are some of the key things you should check before you commit to engaging agencies or freelancers:

- **Have they worked on exactly this kind of project before?** A lot of us like challenges and interesting work, but do you really want to pay for your supplier's learning curve? Although if you doing something truly original there will be some learning to do.

- **Who specifically will be working on the project and what is their experience?** Very often you meet the top consultant but they won't actually be doing the work. I always struggled with this when I worked in the agency environment as I would be pitching the work but somebody else would be delivering it. This meant a project that was signed on the basis of my communication and relationship with someone delivering on the promises I made – all fine when it works but can be difficult when it doesn't. The solution to this is clear and structured briefings and clarity early on about who is doing what.

- **Are they just pushing the work out to a freelancer themselves and marking up the cost?** Although this can also work if they are adding value in terms of project management, communication and quality control.

- **Will they need to interact with other suppliers and are they experienced in doing this?** Ask to see examples of whom they have worked with on what work. This most often happens when design and development are done by different companies/individuals. My best advice on this is to assign a lead agency/freelancer who is responsible for the overall project. This means they must make sure all parties have the correct communications, adhere to deadlines and attend the relevant meetings. This will save you a lot of administrative work as well making someone responsible for ensuring everyone knows what is going on.

- **How much are they willing to do to pitch for your work?** An individual or company that goes the extra mile in the pitch is hungry for the work and will generally pay you more attention when you are a client. By the extra mile, I mean the pitch you receive should not be generic.

- **What happens if you can't agree on design?** The problem with design work is that it can be subjective in part, so discuss what will happen if, after you have signed up, they can't come up with a design that you like. Generally, the agreement you sign will offer you a number of design concepts to choose from. Make sure this is clear, and then see how much the design of choice can be tweaked and changed. Is this limited in the contract? You can find yourself in an endless loop of design tweaks that lead to a very average design. Choose a designer who has produced work you like, has studied design professionally and thoroughly understands usability – then let them do their job. Unfortunately, most designs are ruined by one of two things: they were no good in the first place, or they started off well and then one or more people on the client side made changes until there was nothing interesting left. If there is no one in your organization (whether you or someone else) with a professional under-standing of design, then don't act as if there is! It's amazing how many MDs and CEOs feel they are experts in web design!

- **What are the timescales? What happens if the agency/freelancer misses their deadlines? What are your responsibilities and when do they need to be delivered? What happens if you miss your deadlines?** I generally look to add a clause to any contract that gives you a discount if the supplier misses the deadline by more than an agreed amount. This will depend on you signing things off and providing content at the appropriate time but it serves to make sure the supplier sets a realistic schedule in the first place.

Finding agencies and freelancers

The best way to find an agency in my opinion is via personal recommenda-tion. Social networks make this increasingly easy to do and it's my favourite use of LinkedIn. If you don't have direct social connections with experience in the right type of work, look at options like LinkedIn groups. There are many very active digital marketing discussion groups where you should be able to get several opinions. My general experience is that you need to find the balance between an agency that is big enough to service your needs but is small enough to be hungry for your work. It's never good being a small client for a big agency.

Finding freelancers has become increasingly easy thanks to great websites like UpWork.com. These sites allow you to set your requirements and the freelancers to pitch for your work. You can review their previous work, feedback from other clients, and see how many jobs they have completed, along with average feedback ratings. I love UpWork and have built relation-ships with several developers around the world that I use for all of my development projects now.

Native apps vs web apps

Let's start by discussing some key options we have when approaching the development of an app. A 'native app' is one that is developed for a specific mobile platform, such as iOS for Apple devices or Android-powered devices. We've taken a look at the adoption levels of these devices in various global markets in Part One of this book, and we'll explore the various platforms further in a moment. The key thing to understand is that when you are building an app in this way, you need to develop a different version of the app for each platform.

Web apps, however, have the advantage that they will work on any mobile device that has a suitable browser and language support. Web apps are generally created using HTML5, and the majority of smartphones and tablets support HTML5 apps. So on initial inspection we may think that the obvious choice is a web app, as we only need to create one version. Unfortunately, it definitely isn't that simple and there are quite a few factors to consider.

Web connection

Firstly, web apps very often rely on having some form of internet connection. It is possible to create web apps that give functionality when disconnected from the web; however, this doesn't have the same level of flexibility that native apps can achieve. Don't forget, though, that plenty of native apps like Google Maps also require an internet connection to function properly.

Device functionality

Increasingly, web apps are able to utilize lots of the mobile device features we take for granted in native apps, like geographic location and things like access to cameras. However, this varies from platform to platform, the device being used and the browser on that device. This makes things a little more limited and complex on web apps.

Performance

Native apps offer better performance, speed and a smoother user experience generally. This makes them much better suited to apps that need fast graphics processing or screen swiping. For this reason, there aren't that many successful web app-based games.

Cost

Web apps are generally a lot cheaper to produce than native apps. The development process is easier and you don't have a submissions process as with the native platforms.

Security

Native apps are generally more secure than web apps, due to the control and procedures put in place by the main app stores. This also means that users see these stores as more trustworthy. Users are also less familiar with web apps and therefore have built less trust in this approach.

Monetization

The app stores make it easy to sell your apps and there are various advertising and subscription options available as standard. Therefore, native apps are generally easier to monetize. Web apps need to rely on taking payment in similar ways to a website, and this adds a barrier to payment as users very often will not want to enter credit card details into an app, or may not be willing to use a third-party payment system like PayPal, because of a lack of trust in the web app.

Updates and maintenance

It is much easier to update and maintain a web app, as there is no store you need to submit to, and development is generally quicker and easier than for native apps.

In conclusion, web apps offer some great advantages in terms of development costs and speed to market. They also have the distinct advantage of creating an app once for delivery on multiple platforms. However, these advantages are often outweighed by the disadvantages and limitations of what can currently be achieved with a web app. As mobile browsers and operating systems grow in sophistication, this may change, as the lines between native and web apps begin to blur.

Platform wars

We are going to look at key differences between the two core mobile platforms: iOS from Apple and Android from Google, and their app stores. As discussed earlier in Part One, there are other mobile operating systems such as Symbian, Blackberry and Windows Mobile, but the reality is that you need to have a very specific target audience in mind if you are developing for these relatively low-adoption platforms. That last sentence will cause outrage in some quarters, but realistically, when over 94 per cent of global smartphone and tablet operating system market share (NetMarketShare, 2016) is held by these two platforms, you need to have a very good justification to look elsewhere.

Apple has its App Store and Google has Google Play, the name it now uses for where you can buy and download all forms of content, including apps (as well as music, movies, etc). Both app stores and platforms have a lot of similarities, but there are also some key differences.

The iOS operating system and the Apple App Store are owned, controlled and developed solely by Apple. This means they call the shots. Android, although owned by Google, is actually distributed as an open source platform, meaning it can theoretically be used and adapted by anyone. It's also been adopted by the Open Handset Alliance (OHA) which includes big handset manufacturers like Samsung, Sony and HTC.

When you design an app for iOS, you are designing two key formats: an iPhone and an iPad version. When you design and develop for Android devices it's not that straightforward, and in reality your app could be used on any number of differently sized devices. For this reason, you need to make sure your Android developer is experienced in thinking this process through carefully, especially when the range of Android devices is growing so quickly.

The other key difference between the app stores is the submission process. On the Android platform, as long as you meet the guidelines and go through the appropriate processes, you can quite quickly have your app live on Play. However, with the Apple App Store, you have to go through a manual approval process. This can take anything from a few days through to months when things go wrong. In my experience, about 5–10 days is average. The manual reviewers are not only looking for any deviation from the guidelines given by Apple, but also for any bugs or poor user experience. They are also thorough and pretty fussy. This makes a better user experience, but can be frustrating for a new app creator. Always remember, it's better that any issues get identified now rather than by a real user, which in turn could attract negative reviews and kill your app.

Building an app: conclusions

Before you embark on creating your first app, make sure you understand the process and skills involved. Make sure the user experience is second to none, and test your app thoroughly. Always remember that even a great app won't get any traction without great marketing (or a huge amount of luck) and that you need to focus on supporting your app users to get great reviews.

It can be a complicated and frustrating process at times, but there aren't many things as satisfying as seeing your app climb up the app store charts. Good luck!

I'm always fascinated to hear about people's successes and failures in the app world. Tell us about what you've learnt and achieved and we may feature your app on our site and give you that marketing boost you need: http://www.targetinternet.com/mobilemarketing.

Social media and mobile 11

The reality is that over 80 per cent of all social media time is now spent on a mobile device (Sterling, 2016). Social media is also now the primary reason why we are using mobile apps (Khalaf, 2015).

Mobile devices allow us to capture and share our experiences, connect our real-world experiences to our online world and to stay up to date with what's going on around us. Therefore, mobile devices are intrinsically social, and this is why social media is such an important aspect of mobile. Our mobile devices represent the bridge between our real-world lives and our online interactions. This means that social media via mobile devices offers huge potential.

What we need to consider is how to best utilize this social behaviour for our organizations and to help achieve our business objectives without interrupting an individual's private and personal space. Over 65 per cent of Facebook users are at least 'slightly concerned' about privacy issues (YouGov, 2016), which indicates the general awareness of how all of the data we share via social media carries some risks.

User journey and value proposition

Two of the main themes that we discussed in the first section of this book were understanding the user journey and considering our value proposition. These considerations are key to using social media effectively. We need to make sure we understand which social platforms our target audience is using and that when they use these platforms the mobile user experience is fully optimized. We also need to make sure we are providing value via social media and not just posting for the sake of posting.

Content and engagement

Just like all social media, our ability to utilize it effectively will come down to having interesting and useful content to share, and being willing and able to engage in an open and 'non-corporate' way. Because of the personal nature of mobile devices and of social media, a standard 'corporate communications' tone doesn't work. Even in a B2B environment, we are still dealing with individuals and need to apply core social media principles to our communications.

Bear in mind that anybody can blog, post to social media sites and tweet. In fact, many best practice guides say you should tweet up to 14 times a day for maximum impact (Lee, 2014)! You should only do any of these things, though, if you have something interesting to say.

Mobile social media experience

We must consider the fact that the majority of people using social media on mobile devices are using apps to access these platforms (we looked at apps in more detail in Chapter 10). I personally use the Facebook, Twitter, Instagram, Snapchat, Pinterest and LinkedIn apps on my iPhone every day. So what does this particular way of accessing social media mean for mobile marketing? It means that we need to think about the constraints of these apps.

For example, if you post content to Twitter (or Weibo in China), most of the time you will be sharing a link. How does that link display on a mobile device? With over 85 per cent of Twitter users accessing the service via mobile devices (Yeung, 2016), we need to consider the mobile experience of the links we are driving people to. My own tweets split into two core categories: linking to useful content on my site; and linking to useful content on other people's sites. I know that the experience on my site has been fully optimized for mobile users, but is this the case for other sites I am driving people through to?

Another example is using social networks like Facebook and LinkedIn. Generally, in this case we are posting content to try and create engagement, and very often this content will include images. The images may display very well on a desktop-size screen, but how do they look on a mobile? Much of the social network experience is different in a mobile app as opposed to a desktop version. We need to make sure we have considered this in all of our social posts. We have to assume that users will be on a mobile device at some point and therefore make sure everything works in this format.

Social media in China

If you are targeting the huge potential of the Chinese market, or you are working within China, you need to be aware (or probably already are) that social media can, at first sight, look very different to elsewhere in the world. Actually the core principles of content, engagement and transparency all still apply, but you will find yourself using completely different platforms.

In most countries globally the social media platforms are fairly universal (with a few exceptions like Mixi in Japan or VK in Russia), but in China there is no Twitter, Facebook or YouTube. Instead there are local market equivalents. Weibos are microblogs like Twitter and there are several, including Sina Weibo and Tencent Weibo. QQ is the most popular instant messenger and Youku is a popular equivalent to YouTube.

Just as with any market, you need to understand what social platforms your target audience is using and then engage using the right tone and content.

For a great resource on social media in China, and the whole Asia region, take a look at: http://www.techinasia.com/.

Informing your social media approach

There are a number of tools that can help inform and manage our social media activity and make sure we are delivering the right content in the right way.

Using search to inform content themes

Google Trends is a fantastic free tool that allows us to see how users search in Google and the trends in searches over time. The great thing about this tool is that not only can we understand search trends but we can use this to inform our social content. We look at this tool a lot more in Chapter 12 on mobile search, but in this case we are going to use it to find out what people are interested in, in order to inform what we should be talking about on our social platforms. The chart in Figure 11.1 shows searches for the word 'iPhone' over a particular period of time: http://www.google.co.uk/trends.

Figure 11.1 Google Trends: search for the word 'iPhone'

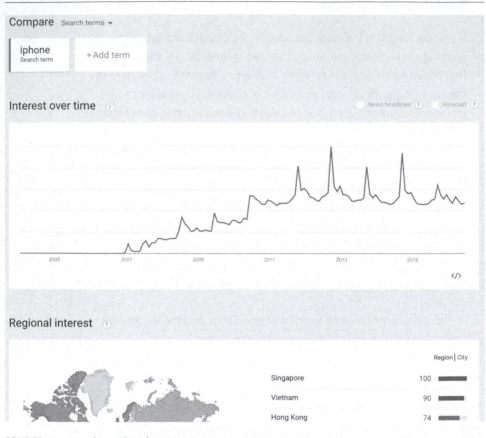

SOURCE: www.google.com/trends
Google and the Google logo are registered trademarks of Google Inc; used with permission

The standard Trends tool will show you relative search volumes over time for a particular word or phrase. We can drill down by time, region, country or language. The tool will try and identify related news stories to points on the graph, showing us geographical interest and the most popular and fastest-rising variations of these search terms.

Probably the most important feature is the ability to compare the trends for different search terms, and this is particularly important for informing content.

Figure 11.2 shows the phrases 'internet marketing' and 'digital marketing' being compared. We can see a decline in interest for internet marketing and a rise in interest for digital marketing. I clearly need to be talking about digital marketing rather than internet marketing on my social platform, because that's what people are searching for and are interested in.

Figure 11.2 Google Trends: word comparison

SOURCE: www.google.com/trends
Google and the Google logo are registered trademarks of Google Inc; used with permission

One thing to be clear about is that Google Trends shows you relative volumes of searches, not the actual numbers of searches. If you want the actual number of searches, you'll need to use the Keyword Tool, and we discuss this in Chapter 12 on mobile search. Relative volumes will show a score of 100 at the peak volume of searches. The rest of the score over time is relative to this. When multiple words are compared, the highest point with a 100 score is the most searched of the words being compared at its highest search volume.

One of the limitations of the Trends tool is its lack of ability to show trends for niche search terms. You'll find in many cases that a niche search term shows that it doesn't have enough data to plot a chart.

Social listening tools

Social listening tools are something that every organization of every size should be using. They allow you to monitor a number of different social channels to look for activity around certain phrases or topics. This capability can be used at a number of stages throughout social media campaigns and these listening tools are essential for effective social media use.

First, these tools can be used in the 'listening' stage, when we are trying to understand what social channels our audience are using, what they are saying, what they are interested in and what our competitors are doing. Many organizations will carry out a listening project before starting any social media activity as part of their standard process before initiating a campaign.

Next, these tools can be used to monitor the effectiveness of social media activity. We can monitor groups of words and phrases to see what is happening on an ongoing basis, and how our audience reacts to our social activity.

Finally, social listening tools can be used to manage outreach and engagement, by identifying key influencers on social channels. This can be important when trying to grow your audience, but also when dealing with negative feedback or a crisis. The idea is to influence the influencers, much like in traditional public relations (PR), but in the case of social media we can do this at a much more granular level.

Some social listening tools also include elements of workflow management, and help you to manage your social media efforts. For example, you may be able to track which social media users you have engaged with, which individual in your organization was involved and plan future activities.

Social media monitoring and listening tools

There is a huge array of social media monitoring tools out there, varying widely in price and capability. At the free end of the spectrum you'll find an enormous selection of tools. However, these tools are fairly limited, and the old adage that 'you get what you pay for' generally holds true. Amongst them are:

- http://www.socialmention.com - one of the better free tools and shows you at a basic level what social monitoring is about. However, like all free tools it is limited in how many sources it looks at and has limited options to segment results by location, etc.

- http://www.brandwatch.com – my favourite social monitoring tool and well worth the cost. Very powerful, flexible and used by some of the world's leading companies.

Social analysis tools

Social analysis tools are different to social listening/monitoring tools in that they generally look at one social platform and give you some analysis or functionality for that particular platform. In fact, many social media sites have these built in. For example, Facebook Insights will give you a range of reports that allow you to see which of your posts were most popular, where the users that like you are in the world, and who is engaging with your content.

There are literally thousands of these tools out there but I have highlighted a few below to give you a flavour of what you can expect. Generally, they will analyse your audience and content and give you some insight into how to take your campaigns forward:

- http://www.tweriod.com – find out the most effective time of day and day of the week to post your tweets.
- http://klear.com/ – analyse social accounts and topics with this excellent free tool (with paid options).
- Facebook Insights – accessed when you have set up a Facebook page, Insights gives you huge insight into what content is working.
- YouTube Insights – another one accessed via the social platform itself, to find out which of your videos are actually getting engagement.
- http://www.followerwonk.com – oddly named and very powerful tool for analysing Twitter audiences.

Figure 11.3 shows an example of the social media analysis tool Klear.com. This Figure shows the tool analysing my Twitter account.

The list could go on and on, so we've compiled and are constantly updating a huge list on the website to accompany this book: http://www.targetinternet.com/mobilemarketing.

Analytics

Your web analytics is one of the most powerful tools for informing your social media activity. You'll not only be able to understand which social media sites are driving traffic to your website, but also how many of these visitors were on mobile devices, and which devices they were using.

We'll explore analytics in a great deal more detail in Chapter 19 on mobile analytics, but it is worth mentioning at this point that analytics can help you understand the impact of your social media campaigns on your broader digital objectives.

Figure 11.3 Analysis of a Twitter account using Klear

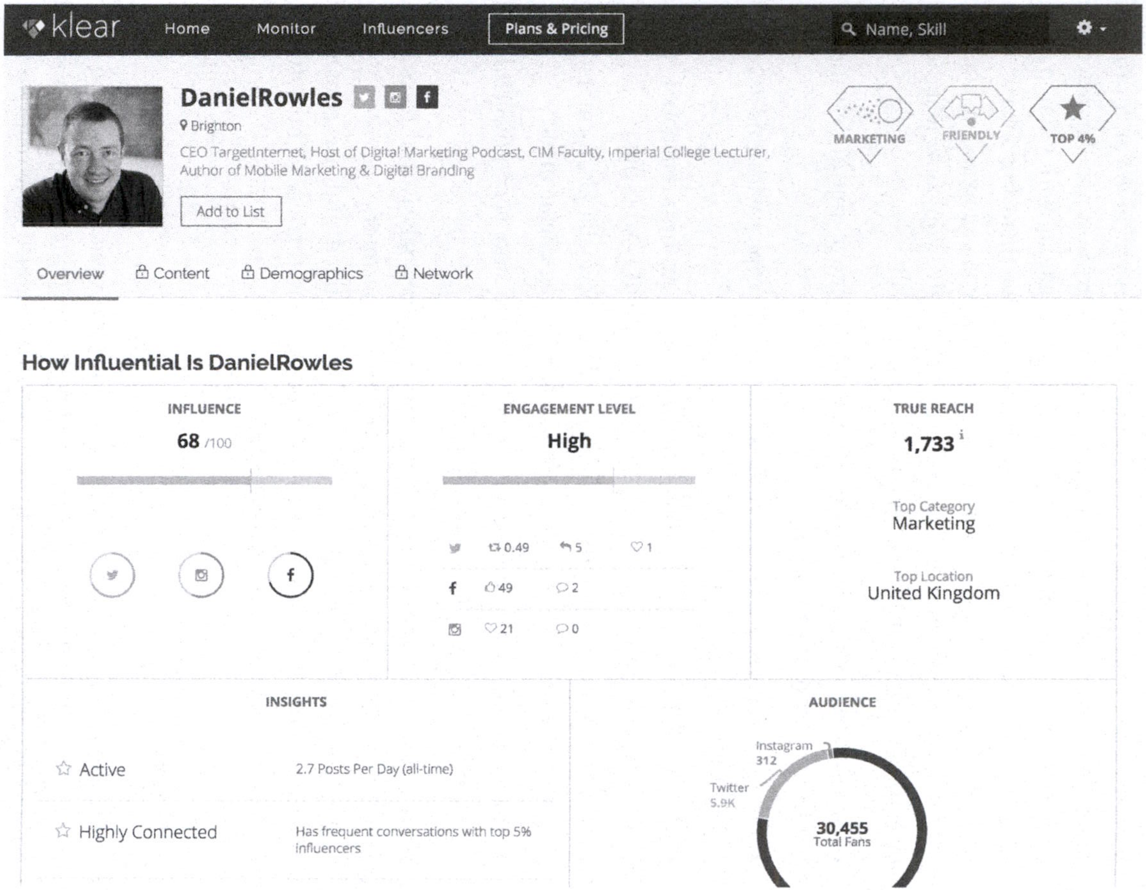

SOURCE: www.klear.com

The importance of Google Analytics

Google Analytics is a powerful and sophisticated web analytics platform that also happens to be free. It has around 83 per cent market share of the entire analytics market (W3Techs, 2016) and is improving and offering more and more functionality all the time. It is suitable for the majority of site owners' needs and offers extensive reports around mobile sites and apps.

There are of course other commercial analytics packages available, and these have the advantage of account managers and service level agreements. Google Analytics Premium does offer these things, but pricing is currently $150,000 annually.

Policy and planning

So you have worked out the kind of content you are going to need and you understand which channels are appropriate for your target audience. You've also thought through the mobile experience and made sure that it is optimized at all stages. So you're ready to start your mobile social media activity? Nope. One of the most important elements of successful social media is having a clear and workable social media policy, and this should have specific considerations for mobile devices.

Social media policies are there to help anyone involved in carrying out your social activity and outline the dos and don'ts of social media within your organization. They will outline things like:

- reporting structure of team involved with social media and clear direction where to seek advice;
- appropriate social media channels;
- guidance on tone of voice;
- guidance on suggested tools, log-ins and who should be using them;
- process for identification and mitigation of risks;
- escalation policy for use when problems are identified;
- responsibilities and legal requirements;
- guidance on suitable content;

- direction on frequency of content posting;
- moderation guidelines;
- best practice on posting mobile-optimized content;
- guidance on creating mobile-optimized landing pages;
- mobile testing platforms;
- guidance on success measures and relevant analytics reports.

Every organization should have its own social media policy and this can help mitigate risks, create effective and consistent social communications and make sure that everyone understands the importance of mobile-optimized content.

Database of social media policies

This site has a huge list of example social media policies you can review to provide insights for your own site. At the time of publishing there were over 300 policies listed: http://socialmediagovernance.com/policies.php.

Outreach, engagement and ego

Although this is not something that is exclusive to mobile social media, we should always consider how we can maximize our reach into our target audience. Social outreach and engagement is a highly effective way of doing this, and as well as increasing the size of our audience it can help us create positive engagement as well.

If I keep on publishing useful and engaging content, regularly update my social channels and positively engage with anyone who leaves comments or feedback, I will gradually grow my social media audience. If, however, I want to speed up this process and create the maximum amplification for my efforts, I am going to need to focus on social media outreach.

Social outreach is all about identifying the key influencers and advocates within a particular group. If I can get these key people to share my updates and content I can amplify my visibility and potentially grow my audience.

So let's define what we mean by an influencer or an advocate:

- **Advocates** are the easiest group to identify as they are the people who leave positive comments, retweet things and generally engage in a positive way. They are willing to spread what you say and add to your social voice. They are our greatest asset and we need to engage, encourage and reward this group to build loyalty.

- **Influencers** are those people with access to the audience we want to influence. We can use social media tools to identify them and we then need a strategy to get engagement and encourage them to become advocates.

Judging influence

You can use a number of measures to judge influence online. You could look at the number of social connections somebody has, or look at the quality of their audience. You could consider how likely it is that what they say will be read and repeated. This process can be quite time-consuming and therefore it is worth considering some of the key tools that can help us understand influence.

Klout, pictured in Figure 11.4, aims to take the pain away from trying to work out influence online. It works by looking at a range of social platforms, assessing over 400 different factors, such as your likelihood of being retweeted, and then gives you a score out of 100. It will also assign topics it believes you are influential about. So from the screen shot you can see I currently have a score of 65 and according to Klout I am influential about social media, mobile marketing and digital marketing (phew!).

Scoring services such as Klout have actually received a lot of negative press and have been accused of everything from inaccuracy through to being nothing more than a way of flattering people's egos. I disagree. Although Klout is far from perfect, as their algorithm (the set of rules behind the scores) improves, so does its effectiveness. There will always be arguments about how much a particular factor or platform should be weighted, but in reality it can give you the rough guidance you need. If I look at all of my Twitter followers and look at those with the highest Klout scores, there is no doubt that these people are my most influential audience.

The key point of Klout is that it gives me a simple metric to initially assess online influence (of an individual or an organization). I can then dig a little deeper and plan my campaigns to reach out to these online influencers. For example, I have a plugin for Google Chrome that shows me the Klout score of all the people whose tweets I am reading on Twitter. That way I can see who is most influential and prioritize my engagement activities.

Figure 11.4 Klout: social media influence scoring platform

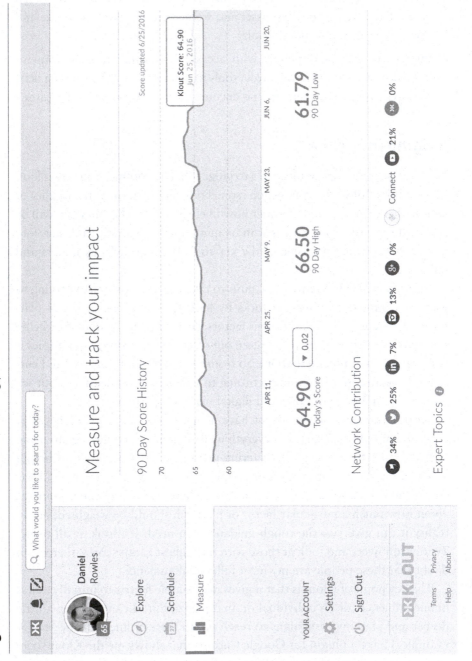

Figure 11.5 Influential Twitter users on the topic of starting a business

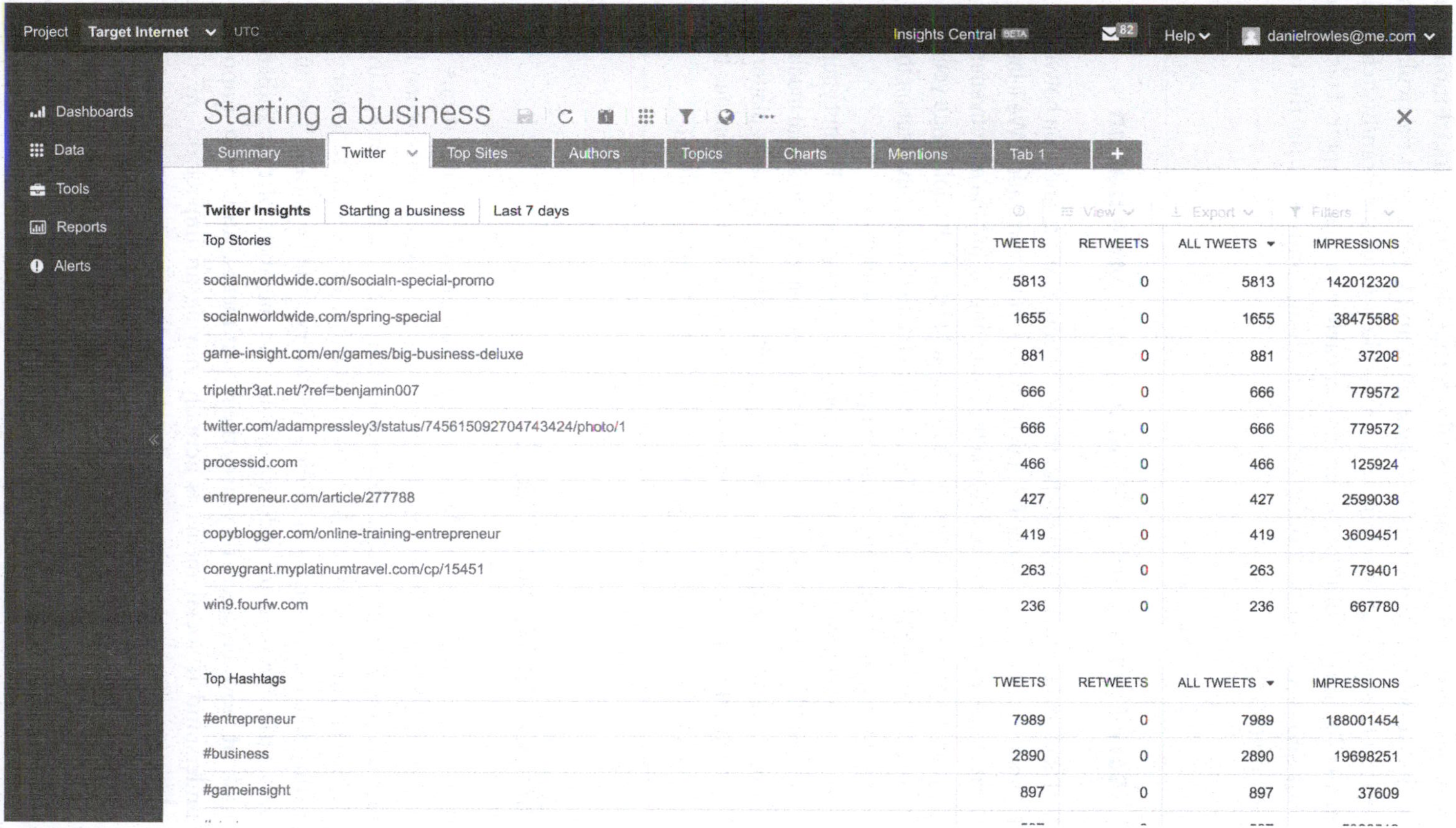
Project
Target Internet
UTC
Insights Central
82
Help
danielrowles@me.com
Dashboards
Data
Tools
Reports
Alerts
Starting a business
Summary
Twitter
Top Sites
Authors
Topics
Charts
Mentions
Tab 1
Twitter Insights
Starting a business
Last 7 days
View
Export
Filters
Top Stories
TWEETS
RETWEETS
ALL TWEETS
IMPRESSIONS
socialnworldwide.com/socialn-special-promo 5813 0 5813 142012320
socialnworldwide.com/spring-special 1655 0 1655 38475588
game-insight.com/en/games/big-business-deluxe 881 0 881 37208
triplethr3at.net/?ref=benjamin007 666 0 666 779572
twitter.com/adampressley3/status/745615092704743424/photo/1 666 0 666 779572
processid.com 466 0 466 125924
entrepreneur.com/article/277788 427 0 427 2599038
copyblogger.com/online-training-entrepreneur 419 0 419 3609451
coreygrant.myplatinumtravel.com/cp/15451 263 0 263 779401
win9.fourfw.com 236 0 236 667780
Top Hashtags
TWEETS
RETWEETS
ALL TWEETS
IMPRESSIONS
#entrepreneur 7989 0 7989 188001454
#business 2890 0 2890 19698251
#gameinsight 897 0 897 37609

SOURCE: www.brandwatch.com

Another approach to judging social influence is to use a social monitoring tool that helps you identify the most influential users on a particular platform. The screen shot in Figure 11.5 is taken from the Brandwatch social media listening tool that we mentioned earlier in this chapter. This screen shot shows the most popular stories, hashtags and users on the topic of 'starting a business'.

Social media, online PR and search optimization

It's important to understand that there is a very close connection between your social media activity, PR activity and search optimization. We'll look at mobile search in more detail in the next chapter, but the effectiveness of your social media activity will create 'social signals' that influence your search rankings (essentially the quantity and quality of conversation that is happening in social media around your topics of interest).

Social engagement and outreach are essentially online PR, but your offline PR activities can also impact what you talk about in social media and how many people are linking to your sites and social media platforms. For this reason, we need everyone involved in these three disciplines to work collaboratively and be aware of what the others are doing.

Social measurement

The greatest mistake made in a huge number of organizations (in my experience the majority) is to focus on volume-based metrics when looking at social media campaigns. More often than not, a campaign is started and the initial target is to reach a certain number of likes or followers. But in reality what does having a million followers actually mean? The answer is very little. We need to understand who the members of that audience are, look at how engaged they are, their sentiments, and, most importantly, understand if social media is actually having an impact on my business objectives.

We'll look at mobile analytics much more in Chapter 19, but we can use analytics to look at the success of our mobile social media activity in a number of ways. We can start with the basics, and look at how much traffic we are getting from social media sites to our websites. We could then take it a stage further and look at how many of these visits are on mobile devices. If we are using analytics effectively, we will have also set up goals, and we can see what part social media, and particularly mobile social media, is having on driving my website visitors to complete my goals. All of this will be covered in more detail in Chapter 19, but the key point is that it's not just about the social media data, like number of followers or amount of engagement: it's actually about understanding how this drives my end objectives.

Benchmarked measurement

One of the key problems with looking at volume-based metrics is that it doesn't give you an indication of what success actually looks like. You may feel that getting 10,000 followers on your Facebook page is a great success. However, if your nearest competitor has 500,000 followers, it's suddenly a very different story. For this reason, we need to try and benchmark our measurement, and there are a couple of ratio-based measures that are easy to use, but very rarely looked at: share of voice and audience engagement.

Share of voice

This is a great ratio for understanding where you sit in relation to your competitors, and for judging the success of and reaction to your social media efforts. You'll need a social media listening tool to calculate this, and for many channels there are free tools that will do the job.

You start by measuring the total level of conversation around the topic area you are concerned with. In my case this would be digital marketing, but it could be anything. For example, a recent client looked at all of the conversations around skincare. The easiest way to do this is to look at channels one at a time, so for example, how many tweets are there around the topic of skincare within a particular geographic region (you can do this using most social media monitoring tools).

You achieve this by deciding on a set of keywords and phrases that you want to monitor, and then see the level of conversation on these phrases. You would then repeat this process, but just identify the tweets that were specifically about, or mentioned, your product, brand or service. You will then have two numbers, one for total conversations and the other for conversations about you. Divide the number of conversations about you by the total number of conversations on the topic, and you have your 'share of voice' percentage.

This may be very low, but you can continue your social media efforts, and then take the measurement on a regular basis (normally monthly is sufficient). Progress made in increasing this percentage gives you a more useful guide than just looking at a number of tweets or likes. The other great thing about this measure is that you can calculate it for your competitors. You then have a benchmarked measure that can give you an indication of how effective your efforts are and how that compares to your competitors.

Sentiment analysis

Many social media tools will carry out some form of sentiment analysis. The idea is that the context of the social media mentions you receive is analysed, and the sentiment or intention of the social media user is understood. This most usually takes the form of grouping these mentions into positive, negative and neutral.

There is a problem, however. The majority of social media tools get this completely wrong. These tools work by analysing the text and using fairly rudimentary methods of analysing the language. For example, if I tweet 'Top 10 digital marketing disasters of 2017' and then link to my website, many tools will see this as a negative tweet and associate negativity with the link to my website. It will be seen as negative due to the use of the word 'disaster'; however, from experience, this will actually be a very popular tweet. Some tools, however, are a lot more effective at analysing language and take a far more sophisticated approach. These tools are certainly not 100 per cent accurate, but they are far less likely to make rudimentary mistakes like this.

The solution is to understand how effective your particular tool is at analysing the social platforms you are looking at, and then manually checking the results you get. This doesn't mean reading every single tweet or comment (although in an ideal world you will), but it certainly means scanning through and understanding the assumption the tool is making.

This is particularly important when you look at share of voice. During a really bad social media crisis, when everybody is talking about you and saying negative things, your share of voice will be high. You therefore need to understand sentiment when you look at share of voice.

Audience engagement

This is another percentage that you can easily measure and benchmark against your competitors. I tend to look at it on a platform-by-platform basis, so I will know my audience engagement for Twitter, Facebook, Instagram, etc and make efforts to improve this. Again, I normally measure this on a monthly basis.

You start by looking at the size of your overall audience on a particular social platform, such as Facebook or Twitter, and then you consider how much of that audience is actually engaging with you. So, for example, if you have 10,000 likes in Facebook, and when you post some content you get 1,000 likes on that piece of content from your likes, your audience engagement is 10 per cent.

We need to define what we mean by 'engagement'. On a platform such as Facebook, there are multiple ways to engage as you can like, share and comment on a post. I would count any of these activities as engagement. With Twitter I consider a reply or a retweet to be engagement, and so on. Now, technically speaking, if the same user were to carry out multiple engagement activities on the same platform on the same piece of content, we should probably not count these more than once. In practice it doesn't actually matter, as long as you are comparing like for like.

As well as taking this measure for your own social platforms, you can very easily analyse your competitors as well.

Benchmarking and business results

Although these benchmarked measures don't relate directly to business results, they are far more connected to helping us achieve our objectives than just looking at volume-based metrics alone. Realistically, if you are targeting the right audience, your share of voice is growing and your audience engagement is increasing, you are in a strong position.

The next stage is to connect these social media measures to our web analytics and business objectives, and we'll look at this in detail in Chapter 19 on mobile analytics.

Social media advertising

Many social media platforms give you a number of paid advertising options. We'll explore these paid opportunities more in the mobile advertising chapter (Chapter 13), but we should explore some of the key issues we need to consider here. Since we have already said that the majority of social media usage is on a mobile device, social advertising is a predominantly mobile form of advertising and pretty much all social channels allow us to target by device type. As well as targeting options we can preview what our ads will display like on mobile devices. For example, the Facebook platform will preview what your ads or 'boosted posts' (more on that in a moment) will look like on a mobile device. However, we need to make sure that we fully consider the mobile user journey before we place any mobile advertising at all.

Value proposition, privacy and trust

Since our mobile devices are in many cases very much part of our personal and social lives, we need to be very cautious about how we use these devices in a blatantly commercial way. Nearly everything we have spoken about so far involves providing value via engagement and understanding the user needs. Exactly the same principle should be applied to social advertising.

We need to consider how much of an interruption social advertising can actually be seen as, how it can actually damage our brands if used badly and what image we are projecting of our organization. Facebook itself is responding to this, and the Facebook algorithm filters out content and target ads to maximize user relevance.

The key point is to understand the social platforms you are using, why a user is there and make sure the value proposition is clear. If you are on Facebook, you are interested in health and fitness, and brands like Nike offer you free tools to help you achieve your fitness goals, then that's great. If, however, you are on Facebook and you have liked a digital marketing podcast, it doesn't mean that any of your friends necessarily have an interest.

The screen shot in Figure 11.6 shows how much of an impact boosting a post in Facebook can have on boosting your audience. In this particular case, boosting my post meant my post was seen by an additional 2,210 people and I gained 995 actions (for a budget of £14). Boosting posts can make your content more visible to people that have already liked you, those people that have liked you and their friends or just to be people you target via options like interests and demographics. Whilst in this particular case this leads to an increase in overall likes and engagement (as well as a knock-on impact in Klout score), what isn't clear is how many people saw my ad for whom it wasn't relevant, and how much of an impact this had on what these people thought of my brand.

Figure 11.6 Facebook: the impact on audience size of boosting a post

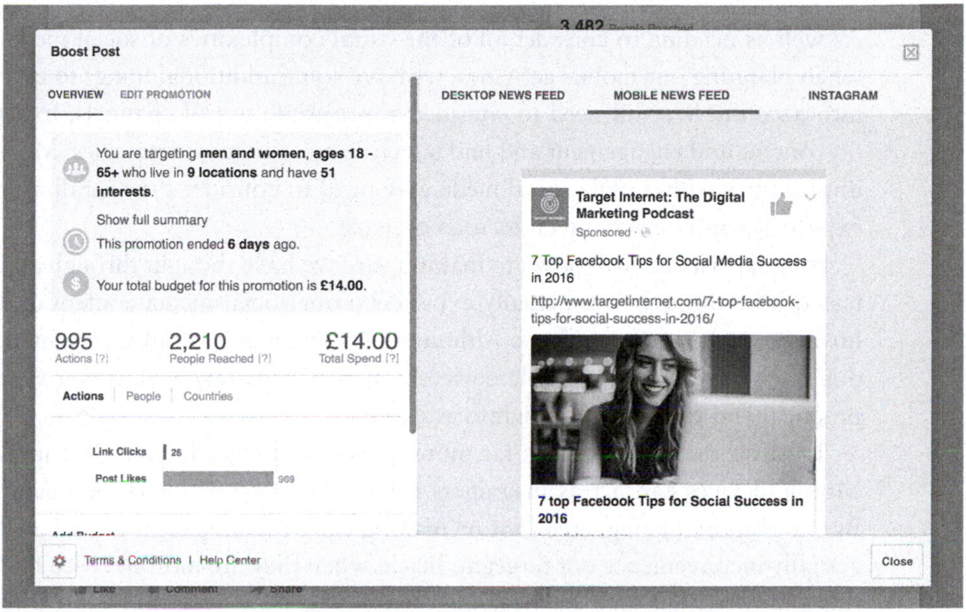

SOURCE: www.facebook.com

Trusting algorithms

The reality is that it's actually in Facebook's interest not to annoy people with irrelevant ads, just as it's not good for Google to give you irrelevant search results. Both scenarios lead to dissatisfied users, which in turn leads to those users moving to other social networks and search engines.

The algorithms, which are just sets of rules and logic, behind these sites are what decide which ads you are shown or which search results you are given. Google has spent many years and much investment in developing its algorithms and focusing on relevancy. For Facebook it's relatively early days, but mobile advertising already represents the majority of their income. As time goes on, the algorithm that targets the advertising is likely to become more advanced and more effective at doing this in a highly targeted way.

Mobile social media: conclusions

As well as needing to consider all of the usual complexities of social media when planning our mobile activities, we have some additional things to take into account. We still need to consider appropriate use of channels, focus on content and engagement and find effective measurement strategies. Most importantly with mobile social media, we need to consider the overall user experience and be very much focused on trust.

User experience is all down to making sure we have thought through and tested how the user will actually experience our social media content and how they can engage with us. Although time-consuming and fragmented, due to the number of possible devices and scenarios involved, it is a very practical and reasonably straightforward issue.

Trust on the other hand is far more subjective but of huge importance. Mobile devices can act as magnifiers for missteps we make as marketers. By interrupting, being irrelevant or making incorrect assumptions, we will actually inconvenience our target audience when they are most likely to find this annoying. This may be by giving them much more irrelevant content to scroll past or bombarding them with the same message again and again.

As with all social media, mobile social can be a double-edged sword: it gives us great opportunity but also carries risks. This means that now more than ever, mobile social media requires well-thought-out and considered plans that focus on providing value to the user.

Mobile search 12

Mobile search is growing phenomenally, with Google reporting over 50 per cent of searches now being on a mobile device and growth in mobile ad revenues increasing more than 20 per cent per year (Meola, 2016). With more and more users relying on mobile searches, mobile search is an essential part of any mobile strategy.

Defining mobile search

We would normally divide search into two key areas: natural or organic search, the area of the search results decided upon by the search engines; and paid search, the set of results that we can pay to be visible in. Search engine optimization (SEO) is the process of achieving search rankings within the natural/organic results. Pay-per-click (PPC) refers to the paid-search element of search results. We'll explore both in this chapter.

SEM: my least favourite three-letter acronym

As you have probably already worked out, we love three-letter acronyms in digital marketing. Of all these acronyms, SEM is my least favourite. It stands for 'search engine marketing', and technically (I'll happily argue till I'm blue in the face over this) speaking, it means both sides of search marketing, that is both SEO and PPC. However, it is often used to describe the paid side of search, PPC. Because of this ambiguity, I won't be using it again in this book!

In reality, we could place PPC within the advertising section of this book, because that's exactly what it is: a form of paid advertising. However, the term 'online advertising' is most often used to refer to banner and video ads, so for the sake of consistency with this definition, we'll discuss PPC within this section of the book.

Desktop vs mobile results

The major search engines, and particularly Google, will try to give a mobile-optimized search experience. Although Google has recently moved towards having a more consistent experience across devices, it still optimizes your results based on your device.

Mobile optimize or die!

Google's algorithm will punish your site, by pushing you down the search rankings, if they do not believe it is mobile-optimized. That could mean, even if you never, ever receive mobile visitors (highly unlikely!) that you still need a mobile-optimized website. Happily, as you can see in Figure 12.1, you can easily check if Google thinks your website is suitably optimized by using the Google Mobile-Friendly tool. www.google.co.uk/webmasters/tools/mobile-friendly/.

The screen shot in Figure 12.2 shows the kind of results you will see when searching for something that includes a location-specific term. The results shown are a mix of paid search (at the very top of the page), followed by a series of results shown on a map and then organic search results. This means that we now have to scroll three screens down to see the organic search results, thus making things even more challenging when optimizing for mobile search (although the map results are actually a form of organic search results). This means that maximizing our chances of showing in the map results is essential.

Most search engines offer some form of local business registration, when your business has some form of physical presence (Figure 12.2). Generally, registering your business within the mapping element of a search engine will help these results. There is also a range of tools that will help you optimize your local listing across the web to help you rank better in local search results.

The screen shot in Figure 12.3 shows customized search results based on the physical location of the user searching. I live in Brighton in the UK, so my results have been optimized to try and show me local results, because

Figure 12.1 Google's Mobile-Friendly test

‹› Google Developers

Mobile Guide Get Started Documentation › Mobile-Friendly Test

Mobile-Friendly Test G+1

http://www.targetinternet.com/   ANALYZE

Awesome! This page is mobile-friendly.

How Googlebot sees this page

Learn more about mobile-friendly pages

If you're interested in learning more about mobile sites, check out our Webmaster's Mobile Guide or the Principles of Site Design on Web Fundamentals.

Do you use Google Search Console?

See how many of your pages are mobile-friendly by signing into your Search Console account.

Give feedback

Encountered an issue with the test? Comments or questions about the results? Post to our discussion group.

SOURCE: www.google.co.uk/webmasters/tools/mobile-friendly/
Google and the Google logo are registered trademarks of Google Inc; used with permission

Figure 12.2 Mobile search: results based on location term

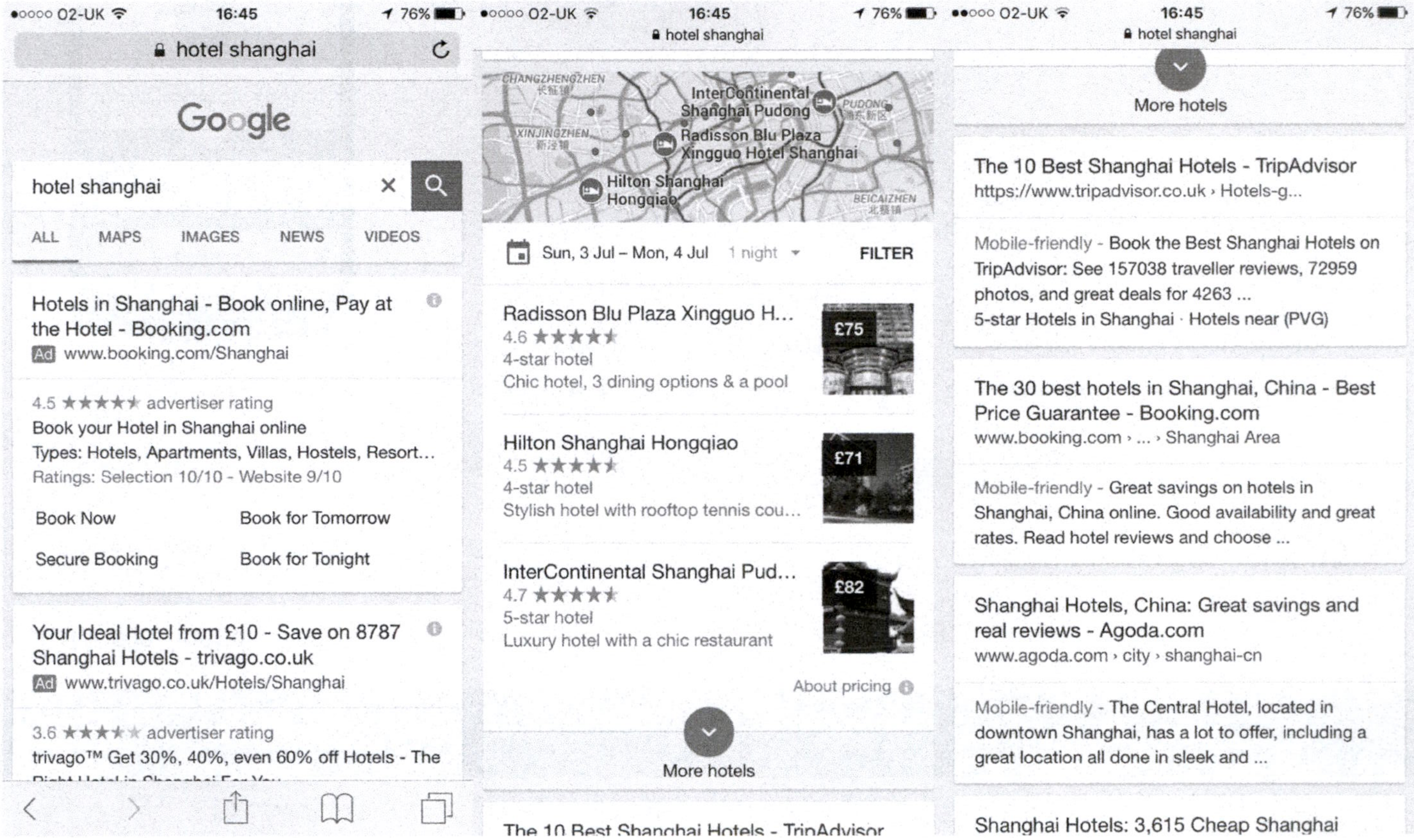

SOURCE: www.google.com
Google and the Google logo are registered trademarks of Google Inc; used with permission

Figure 12.3 Mobile search: results based on user location

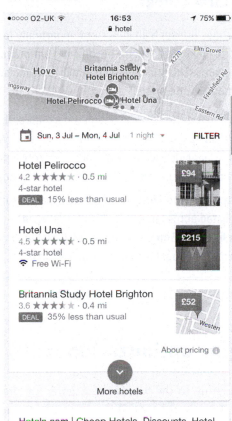

Google has decided the term I am searching for has location-based properties. For this reason, when you are doing your keyword research (a topic we will discuss in more depth shortly) it is important to try your search terms out on a mobile device to see the kind of results you are getting. Again, in this case, making sure I am listed in the map results is important, and paid search is also very visible and is actually shown above the results on this screen shot.

We are able to target PPC advertising specifically at mobile devices, and to give particular functionality to our ads that can help the mobile experience, such as 'click-to-call' buttons. We'll explore the PPC options in more depth shortly, but first we are going to explore how we get to the top of the organic search results.

> ## Maximizing local listings
>
> Because local listings are such an important opportunity for mobile search, we need to make sure we are maximizing our presence in these types of search results. The two tools below will help you show up in more map results, particularly in Google:
>
> - Google My Business: https://www.google.co.uk/intl/en/business/ – this allows you to manage your business listings in Google, which can include both physical locations and brands. To verify a physical location, you can be sent a verification number in the post.
> - Moz Local: https://moz.com/local – Moz Local makes sure your physical locations are listed across a host of directory websites. You'll need your location to be listed on Google or Facebook first, but once set up, this can give an excellent boost to your search rankings.

Search engine optimization (SEO)

SEO is all about getting to the top of the organic results in the search engines. Thankfully the core rules of SEO are consistent across both mobile and desktop searches, and we'll explore these core concepts here. We'll also look at the differences between mobile and desktop search and what you can do to make sure you are maximizing your visibility and therefore your traffic and visitors.

It all starts with spiders

Spiders are bits of software that read your pages and send the content back to the search engines. If they can't read your site, you won't get rankings.

The search engine spiders (also known as 'bots' or 'robots') visit your website, follow the links on your pages and send your content back to the search engine so it can be assessed and ranked. This data is known as the search engine's index. Generally, the more often you update your content and the more important your website is seen as being (we'll cover this 'importance' when we look at link building), the more often the spiders will come back to look at your content.

There are certain practices that can stop the spiders from reading your content in the first place, and clearly, if your website can't be read, you won't get ranked. A good example of this is building your entire site in Flash. Flash is a proprietary technology from Adobe that allows you to build animated and interactive web content. Google and the other search engines find it difficult, or choose not to read the content inside Flash. This basically means the search engine sees the 'box' that contains the content, rather than the content itself. You should also remember that Flash will not work on an iOS device, so it is to be avoided on mobile sites.

Google and some of the other search engine spiders will attempt to visit your site and act as a mobile device to look for a mobile-optimized experience (Google, 2016). Sites that are offering an improved mobile experience are then given a boost within the search rankings. This evidence is somewhat subjective, however, as the spiders can detect a difference between desktop and mobile sites, but cannot determine 100 per cent whether it is an optimal experience.

Google operators

If you want to check that Google is visiting your website and when the spiders last visited, you can use the following technique, known as a Google operator. Go to Google as normal, but instead of searching for a word or phrase, type the following into the search box: cache: www.yourwebsite.com.

This will bring back a copy of your website and some details that tell you when Google last visited your site. If this returns nothing it may mean that Google isn't visiting your website.

Google Search Console

For some real insight into how Google's spiders are accessing your pages and any problems they may be having, you need to set up Google Search Console (formerly known as Webmaster Tools). You can find Google Webmaster Tools here: http://www.google.com/webmasters/tools/.

You'll need a Google account to set things up (you can set one up in a couple of minutes) and you'll then need to prove that you own the website you want to get some details on. Google provides step-by-step instructions, but you will need to be able either to edit your web pages' code or to create a new page with a specific name (as this demonstrates to Google that you control the website).

Once installed, Google Webmaster Tools do the following:

- **Get Google's view of your site and diagnose problems** – you can see how Google crawls and indexes your site and learn about specific problems they're having accessing it. Probably the most important feature in regard to what we've been talking about.

- **Discover your links and query traffic** – you can view and download data about internal and external links to your site with the link-reporting tools. Find out which Google search words/phrases drive traffic to your site, and see exactly how users arrive there.

- **Share information about your site** – this allows you to tell Google about your pages with Sitemaps: which pages are the most important to you and how often they change.

It also has some features that allow you to see how fast your pages load in comparison to other sites. This is important as it is one of the factors that Google considers when deciding your rankings.

Keyword research for SEO

Keyword research is all about understanding how your potential audience searches so you know what search phrases you need to rank for. Once we've done this we need to look at getting the words onto our pages, and we'll cover this when we discuss on-page optimization.

It's too easy to make assumptions about what words and phrases our potential audience is searching for based on our own opinions (or possibly the opinions of our search agency). We need to back this up with real facts, and happily there are plenty of free tools that allow us to do just this.

Keyword challenges

Some of the everyday challenges you'll face in keyword research are best demonstrated by giving an example. When I ran a search agency we had a large recruitment client whose basic brief was: we want to be No. 1 for the word 'jobs'. What they were basically asking for was to be ranked first out of about 3,600,000,000 (just search for a phrase in Google on a desktop/laptop and you'll see, just above your search results, the approximate number of pages that Google has in its index containing the searched phrase). We did it (and they are still in the top five) but was this worth the effort and cost?

Generic search terms

Achieving No. 1 positions for broad and generic search terms like this just won't be achievable for most of us (at least in the short term). We won't have the resources (financial or time) to achieve this. In reality we'd also be wasting a lot of time. Who searches for the word 'jobs'? It's most likely to be someone that's assessing the marketplace of recruitment websites. They're at the browsing stage of the online journey and are probably pretty unlikely to be applying for a job on this first visit. In reality if we start by saying, 'I want to be No. 1 for *digital marketing jobs London*,' we start to target people nearer the point of conversion (when they are actually going to do something) and we're going to be competing against a lot fewer people (588,000 in this particular case, which is a lot better than billions!).

So why would a large organization like the recruitment website I mentioned go for such a generic search term? There are a few reasons outlined below:

- **Ignorance** – they may not know very much about SEO.

- **Long term** – it's valid to approach more generic terms in the long term. It's achievable if you're willing to keep working at it and it can make up part of a mixed keyword strategy (this is when you target lots of phrases with lots of combinations of phrases on a topic).

- **Volume** – if you sell online advertising you may be more interested in volume than quality. This is because online ads are generally sold CPM (cost per mille or, basically, cost per thousand views). So, advertisers are charged each time a page is loaded, without taking into account the type of user loading the page.

Long-tail search

The more specific the phrase we search on, the clearer we are on what we are looking for and the more likely a search is to lead to an action. Some form of action, like a purchase, download, application, etc is what we generally want to achieve as marketers, so these longer, or 'long-tail', phrases are what we should often focus on. The phrase 'long-tail' comes from the idea that there is a wide selection of search phrases made up of multiple words that will not drive huge volume (although using multiple long-tail phrases can drive lots of traffic), but are more likely to drive conversion.

Keyword variations

We also need to understand exactly how people search and the order and variations of words that they use. Google wants to match exactly what you've searched for, so the difference between 'jobs Manchester' and 'Manchester jobs' is important. Which variation do most people search on? Luckily Google provides tools that can tell us exactly this, and the two main tools are discussed below.

Keyword Planner

The Keyword Planner is great for finding the actual number (or at least a fairly accurate estimate) of searches for a particular term, which can be looked at globally or country by country. This tool also shows suggested variations of the search term and how many searches these get per month, so it's a fantastic tool for building a list of words for which we want to optimize our pages. Always look at the volume of searches vs how competitive the search term is going to be. The easiest way to do this is just to search the term and see how many results come back in Google: the higher the number, generally the more competition there will be.

One important thing to note about the Keyword Planner from a mobile perspective is that it allows you to separate mobile from overall searches at a high level. You can do this by selecting 'mobile trends' or 'breakdown by device' from the drop-down on the chart at the top of the page (see Figure 12.4).

The screen shot in Figure 12.5 shows the results when looking at the phrase 'mobile marketing'. We are given the number of searches per month globally or locally (if we set to a particular location) and a selection of other related search terms.

Google Trends: http://www.google.com/trends

Google Trends can tell us quite a lot about how people search, but its key capability is in showing trends over time and comparing search terms. Enter a search term and it will show you the trend over time of people searching for that term. It doesn't show an actual number of searches, but rather the trend (the Keyword Planner tells us actual numbers). We can also enter multiple terms and see how they compare. Its other key capability is to show geographical interest in a term by country, which can then be drilled down to by region and city. Always remember that when two countries are compared, it is showing where somebody is more likely to be searching, not

Figure 12.4 Selecting mobile trends in the Keyword Planner

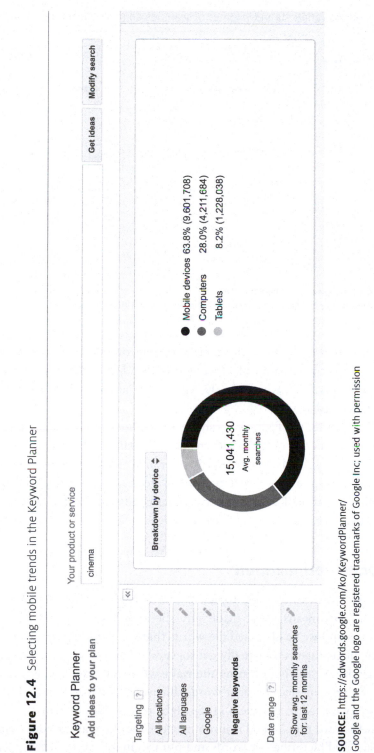

SOURCE: https://adwords.google.com/ko/KeywordPlanner/
Google and the Google logo are registered trademarks of Google Inc; used with permission

Figure 12.5 Keyword variations and volumes of searches on mobile devices

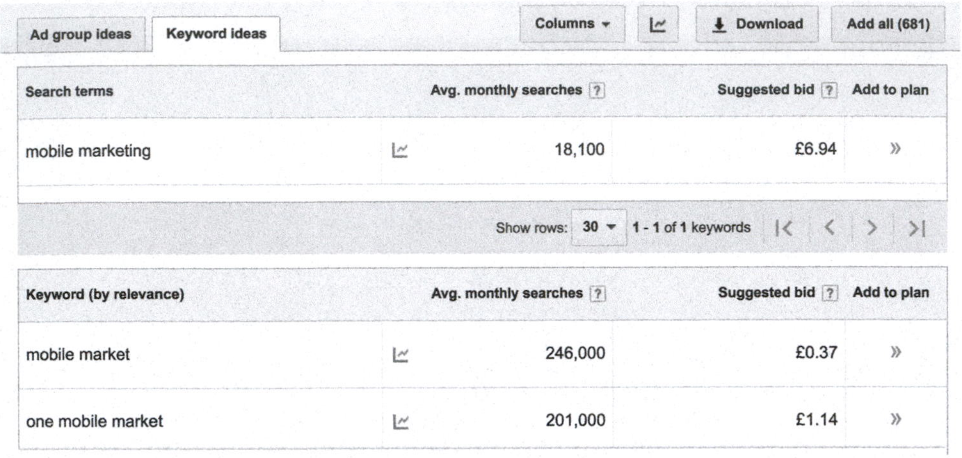

Ad group ideas	Keyword ideas		Columns ▾	⌁	⬇ Download	Add all (681)

Search terms		Avg. monthly searches ?	Suggested bid ?	Add to plan
mobile marketing	⌁	18,100	£6.94	»

Show rows: 30 ▾ 1 - 1 of 1 keywords |< < > >|

Keyword (by relevance)		Avg. monthly searches ?	Suggested bid ?	Add to plan
mobile market	⌁	246,000	£0.37	»
one mobile market	⌁	201,000	£1.14	»

SOURCE: http://adwords.google.co.uk/o/Targeting/Explorer
Google and the Google logo are registered trademarks of Google Inc; used with permission

necessarily that there is actually a larger volume of searches in that country. Finally, we get a selection of other words that have been searched on in relation to this term, which are the most popular, and which have grown most in the past year.

This screen shot in Figure 12.6 shows the comparison of the search terms 'nokia', 'blackberry' and 'iphone' in the UK market. We can see a direct correlation between the market for these brands and the volume of searches for them. Also remember that bad news stories, such as the 'Blackberry blackout', when the Blackberry network stopped working for a number of days, will also cause a peak in searches.

On-page optimization

So far we have explored the topics of search engine spiders and keyword research. This means we've made sure the search spiders can access our web pages and we've identified the words that we want to achieve rankings for. The next stage is to actually get these words onto our pages. On-page optimization is all about getting the right words on the page, in the right place. We've identified the right words during the keyword research phase, and now we need to put them in the right places. This is actually a fairly straightforward process and is just a matter of looking at the core elements of a page and factoring our words and phrases in.

Figure 12.6 Google Trends: comparing search terms

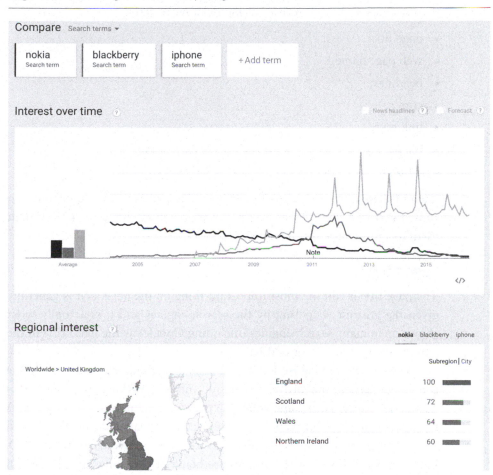

SOURCE: www.google.com/trends
Google and the Google logo are registered trademarks of Google Inc; used with permission

Users first, then search engines

What we are trying to do is help the search engines understand the content on our web pages. However, we don't want to do this at the expense of the user journey. What I mean is that if we over-optimize our content it will actually make our copy hard to read. You can drive all the traffic in the world, but if everybody leaves when they start trying to read your content, you've wasted your time. Focus on getting things right for the user first and then we'll adapt things as appropriate for the search engines.

I've listed below the key areas of the page that are of most importance and then we'll look at each of these elements in more detail:

- page title;
- web page names;
- headings;
- copy;
- link text;
- file names;
- alt text.

Each of these different parts of your web pages gives us the opportunity to show the search engines what the pages are all about. So let's take a look at them in a little more detail (see Figure 12.7).

Page title

The page title is still the most important thing on the page as it is generally given the greatest weighting by the search engines and it is actually what shows up in many search engines (including Google) as the main title in the search engine results pages (SERP).

The page title (see Figure 12.8) is actually something that shows up in the top bar or tab of your browser window, and is something that most users don't even notice when using your web pages. It's actually something that is initially written by your web developer or content management system, and is one of the most commonly missed and most effective elements of SEO. Huge numbers of website page titles are blank or say things like 'home'. In other cases, people repeat the same page title again and again or use their company name. If I am looking for your company name that's fine, but what about when I am searching for what you do? A good page title factors in a range of phrases that a user may search for.

So for example 'online digital marketing training from Target Internet' is a much better page title than 'Target Internet' as it says what my site actually offers and includes the words and phrases that a user might actually search for.

Headings

The headings and subheadings throughout your pages help the search engines to understand the key themes of these pages. Again, these should factor in the most important words and phrases that a user may be searching for and that you have identified during your keyword research.

Figure 12.7 Search engine optimization: key elements of the page

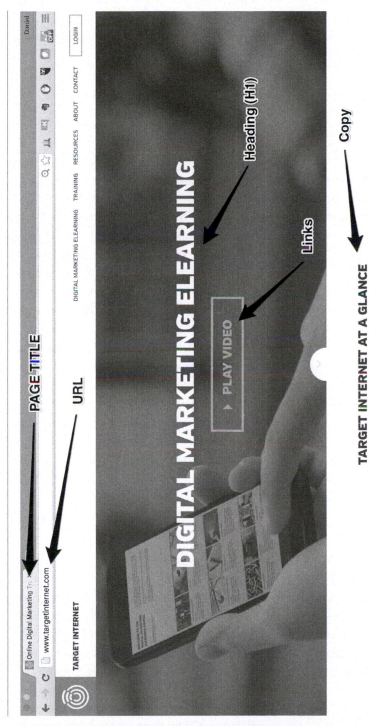

Figure 12.8 Page title: main line of the Google search result

---

Online Digital Marketing Training/Elearning and the Digital Market…
www.targetinternet.com/ ▾
Free **Digital Marketing Elearning**, Training and Resources - Home of the Digital
Marketing Podcast, the Blog of Digital Marketing Consultant Daniel Rowles and …
Digital Marketing Podcasts · Digital Marketing Blog · Contact · Daniel Rowles

Google and the Google logo are registered trademarks of Google Inc; used with permission

The spiders are actually reading the code of your pages rather than looking at the code as we do. The headings in your copy are represented as 'H' tags. These are parts of the HTML code that go to build your pages, and you actually have up to six different tiers or heading tags. The H1 tag is your main heading, the H2 tag is for subheadings and so on all the way through to H6. In reality we most often don't get past using H1s and H2s, which is absolutely fine from an SEO perspective. It's important to understand, though, that you should only ever have one H1 but you can have multiple H2s. The logic behind having only one H1 is so that you are clearly indicating the core theme of your page. Multiple H1s would water down this core theme and make it harder for the search engines to understand the real focus of your page. This is a common mistake and should be avoided.

Bear in mind that the actual part of your page that is used as an H1, H2, etc will be decided either by the person who originally coded your page or by the content management system (CMS) that you are using. For this reason, it may be necessary to have the code of your pages modified to use the appropriate part of the page as heading tags. Thankfully in systems such as WordPress this is all taken care of for you in a very sensible way.

Web page names

Your website address and the actual names of the pages that you create will again act as indicators for the search engines as to what your content is about. This doesn't mean your actual website name must include your keywords, but it does mean that you should name your pages appropriately. For example, my website doesn't have to be called www.mobilemarketing. com if that is the topic of the content (although in an ideal world it would be), but if I create a page on this topic I should name it www.mywebsite. com/mobile-marketing. This is because the search engines are realistic in realizing that many of our websites' addresses are actually our company names and so on. Again, this may be impacted by your original developer or CMS, and systems like WordPress allow you to control this easily.

Copy

The main copy on your pages should include your targeted key phrases, ideally in the first paragraph. However, you certainly don't need to keep repeating the words again and again. In fact, if you do keep repeating the words, not only can you make the copy hard to read, it could actually be interpreted as negative by the search engines (see the box below on 'black hat SEO').

Black hat vs white hat SEO

What we are talking about is ethical, or so called 'white hat', SEO. This means we are trying to help the search engines to understand our content. There is also something called 'black hat' SEO that is all about trying to manipulate the search engines. If you get caught using black hat techniques you can get completely removed from some search engine results, and Google is particularly effective at detecting these techniques.

The main rule is that the website content should be there for the user and not the search engines and that what the user is shown is what the spiders should also see. If you want to understand more about what Google expects and considers to be best practice, you can take a look at their webmaster guidelines: http://www.google.com/webmasters/.

Link text

The actual words that we choose to create the link from on our web pages help the search engine understand the relevance of the page we are linking to (and also help set the context of the page we are linking from to some extent). These actual words we are using to link are referred to as 'anchor text', and it's an important indicator for the search engines. For this reason, we shouldn't use phrases such as 'click here' or 'read more' as these are essentially meaningless to the search engines. These types of phrase also make it harder for a user scanning your page to quickly identify its core themes.

File names

Although only a small factor, the names of the files that make up your pages have some impact on the search engines' understanding of your web pages. So you should name your images, video files, etc appropriately to describe their content and where possible factor in your key words and phrases.

Alt text

Alt text is text that describes an image and is put in place by a developer or when using a CMS. The alt text is there for accessibility reasons primarily, but also has an impact on SEO. Accessibility is all about making your website usable by people who need to use it in a different way for some reason. For example, if I am blind, in order to use the web I will use something called a screen-reader. A screen-reader is a piece of software that reads out web pages in a simulated voice. When this reader gets to an image, it can't understand that image so it reads out the alt text instead. The search engines have a similar problem and don't understand images either. For this reason, they then read the alt text to better understand the image.

As I have said, the alt text is actually for accessibility and SEO should be a secondary consideration. However, if you can factor your keywords and phrases into these descriptions, it does help with your overall SEO efforts. You should also be aware that effective use of alt tags is very important and is actually a legal requirement within the European Union under the Disability Discrimination Act. Wherever you are based, however, alt tags are important to help people access your website, and they have an impact on SEO.

On-page optimization in perspective

Once you've been through the process of identifying your most important words and phrases, and you have made sure they have been put into your pages in the appropriate places, you have done the fundamentals of on-page optimization. The search engines get smarter and smarter about understanding how different topics and themes are interconnected, and Google in particular is getting very good at understanding the context as well as the words of a particular piece of content. For this reason, you shouldn't obsess over on-page optimization too much, but rather focus on providing value through your content. That leads us into the extremely important next step in SEO: link building.

On-page optimization and responsive sites

Always remember that the elements of the page that display on a responsive site will have a fundamental impact on your on-page optimization of that page. There is increasing evidence that the search engines are looking at how our devices display on different devices and are judging the content accordingly. Each of the various page elements is still important, but we need to look at how they differ on each device.

Link building

If on-page optimization is telling the search engines what your content is about, link building is telling the search engines the authority of that content. A link to your content from somewhere else is basically seen as a vote of confidence. People only link to content they find useful or interesting, and therefore links are essential to your search optimization efforts.

Neither on-page optimization nor link building can work in isolation, as both are needed to understand the topic and authority of your site and its content. Driving more links to increase your authority is all about creating engaging and interesting content, and this is one of the reasons why 'content marketing' has become such an important approach in recent years. If our websites just say how great we are or how great our product is, there is little reason for anyone to link to us. However, if we provide value via our content, we are encouraging links, building value and potentially driving engagement.

For example, my own website's primary commercial aim is to drive enquiries for an online training product, but the majority of the site's content is actually all about giving free digital marketing advice. This free advice takes the form of blog posts, podcasts and reports. All of this content drives links from other websites where people find this content useful or interesting, and in turn drives my site up the search rankings.

Link building and mobile sites

In most cases many links you get from other sites won't actually link to your mobile site. This will be particularly true if you are using some form of responsive site, as there may be no mobile-specific URL and the site only becomes a mobile site when the browsing device is detected. Don't worry about this at all. Focus on creating content that drives links; this will then be interpreted by the search engines in the appropriate way.

Social signals

As well as looking at the number of links to our content we have from other sites, the search engines are increasingly concerned with what we call 'social signals'. These social signals are the conversations that are happening in social media about your site and content. This is not to say that you can tweet about your own site a thousand times, and you'll suddenly leap to the top of the search rankings! In Chapter 11 we looked at the social scoring service Klout that attempts to score the social influence of a particular user or social media account. In reality the major search engines have an internal process that works in a similar way, and they are trying to access both the quantity and quality of social signals that are being created about your content.

This increasingly means that using social media to get users discussing, engaging with and sharing your content is highly important. Sharing your latest content with the appropriate social platforms can not only create social signals but also encourage further links to your content.

Measuring link authority

There are a number of tools and methods for measuring how effective our link building strategies are and how authoritative our sites are seen as being. All of these are actually looking at two key things: the quality and quantity of links and social signals to our content.

Search engine algorithms

Much of what SEO agencies concern themselves with is understanding the algorithms the search engines use to decide how your content is ranked in the search results. In my opinion this is increasingly a waste of time. The smarter the search engines get, the more complex their algorithms become and the more of a nonsense it becomes trying to decode this set of rules. I was actually told by somebody at Google that in reality, even within Google, there would only be a handful of people who know and understand the complete set of rules because it is such a complicated and huge thing. Rather than focusing on trying to outwit the engineers at Google (good luck with that!), we should focus on the fundamental issue of creating useful and engaging content.

Open Site Explorer

The first of the tools we'll look at is the excellent Open Site Explorer tool from Moz.com (see Figure 12.9). Moz.com offers a huge range of SEO tools as part of its paid monthly subscription. You can also access Open Site Explorer in a limited way for free. It doesn't give you all of the features, results are limited and you can only use it three times in any one day, but it's still fantastically useful.

When you enter a website or particular web page into the tool it gives you a range of information about the quantity and quality of links to that page. You are given a score out of one hundred for the authority of your domain as well as any particular page you are looking at. It's a great way of benchmarking yourself, and you can do the same for your competitors. The paid version will also show some data on social signals from a limited number of social sites.

Mobile SEO: conclusions

So, just like SEO in general, we can sum up mobile SEO into some fairly straightforward key steps:

- spiders – make sure that your content is visible to the search engines;
- keyword research – understand what your target audience is searching for and build a list of words and phrases that you would like to rank for;

Figure 12.9 Open Site Explorer from Moz.com

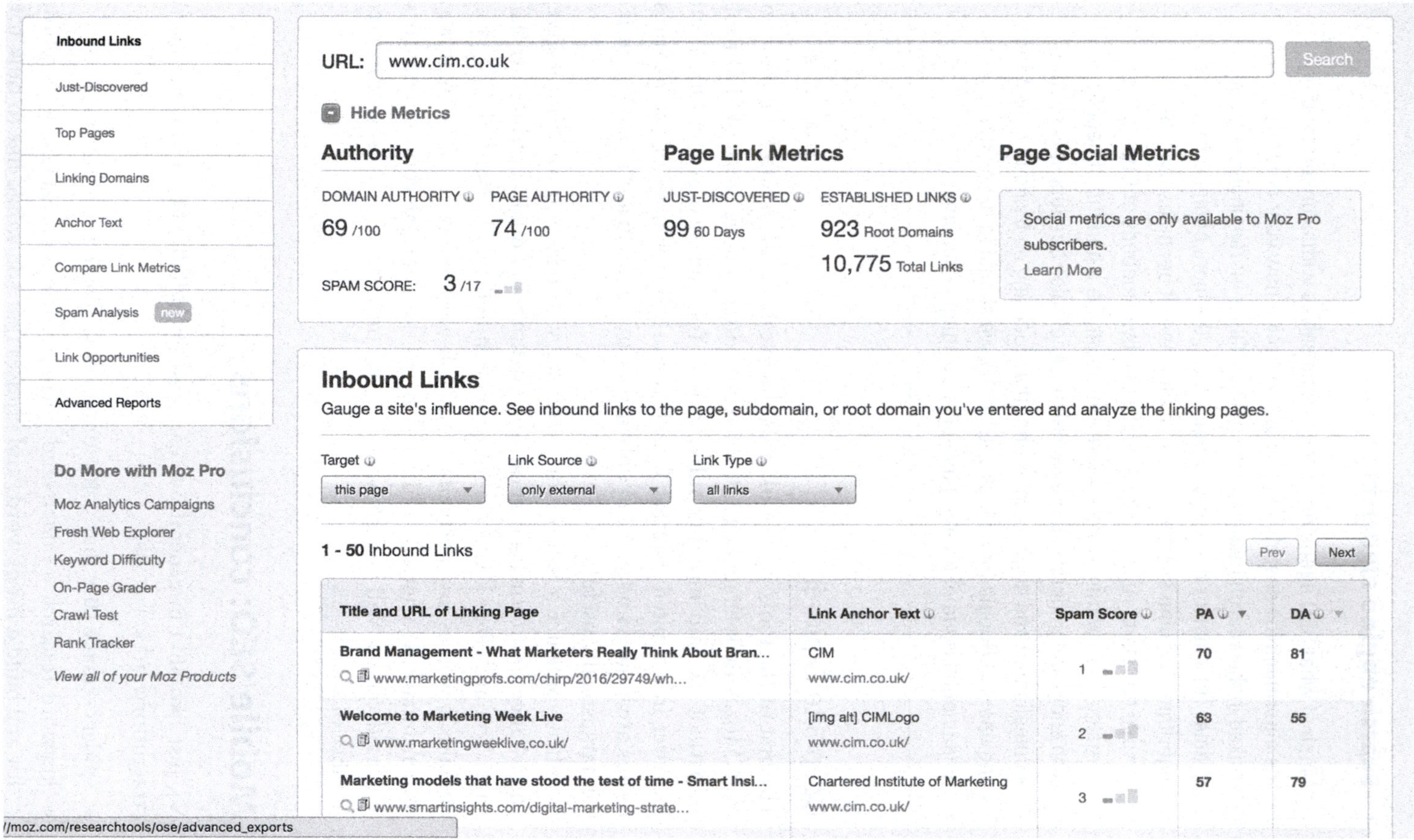

Inbound Links

Just-Discovered

Top Pages

Linking Domains

Anchor Text

Compare Link Metrics

Spam Analysis [new]

Link Opportunities

Advanced Reports

Do More with Moz Pro

Moz Analytics Campaigns

Fresh Web Explorer

Keyword Difficulty

On-Page Grader

Crawl Test

Rank Tracker

View all of your Moz Products

URL: www.cim.co.uk

☐ Hide Metrics

Authority

DOMAIN AUTHORITY ⊕	PAGE AUTHORITY ⊕
69 /100	74 /100

SPAM SCORE: 3 /17 ▁▃▅

Page Link Metrics

JUST-DISCOVERED ⊕	ESTABLISHED LINKS ⊕
99 60 Days	923 Root Domains
	10,775 Total Links

Page Social Metrics

Social metrics are only available to Moz Pro subscribers.

Learn More

Inbound Links

Gauge a site's influence. See inbound links to the page, subdomain, or root domain you've entered and analyze the linking pages.

Target ⊕	Link Source ⊕	Link Type ⊕
this page ▸	only external ▸	all links ▸

1 - 50 Inbound Links

Prev   Next

Title and URL of Linking Page	Link Anchor Text ⊕	Spam Score ⊕	PA ⊕ ▾	DA ⊕ ▾
Brand Management - What Marketers Really Think About Bran... ⊕ 🔍 www.marketingprofs.com/chirp/2016/29749/wh...	CIM www.cim.co.uk/	1 ▁▃▅	70	81
Welcome to Marketing Week Live ⊕ 🔍 www.marketingweeklive.co.uk/	[img alt] CIMLogo www.cim.co.uk/	2 ▁▃▅	63	55
Marketing models that have stood the test of time - Smart Insi... ⊕ 🔍 www.smartinsights.com/digital-marketing-strate...	Chartered Institute of Marketing www.cim.co.uk/	3 ▁▃▅	57	79

/moz.com/researchtools/ose/advanced_exports

Search

SOURCE: www.opensiteexplorer.org

- on-page optimization – get these words on your page in the right places;
- link building – build a content-based strategy to encourage links to and discussions around your content;
- benchmarking – measure and improve your SEO efforts.

The additional steps you need to consider specifically for mobile SEO are:

- mapping and location-based listings – make sure you are listed and have fully registered your site with any location-based services including mapping sites and things like Google My Business;
- mobile site auditing – make sure your mobile site on-page elements are in line with the key themes of your content.

Paid search

Pay-per-click (PPC) is the other side of search, and due to the limitations of screen space in mobile search, it is even more visible and dominates more of the available screen space than in desktop search. We'll look at the pros and cons of PPC in detail, but its key advantage is our ability to control and target it precisely.

If you receive a promise of a No. 1 search ranking from an agency or freelancer, one of two things is happening. They are either talking about PPC, or they are lying! Nobody can guarantee No. 1 rankings in Google, even somebody who has done it a thousand times before, because only Google control it.

Within the major PPC systems we are able to target particular ads at mobile users. This means we control what ads are seen on mobile devices and can change the content shown in these ads accordingly. Want to promote an app? Add a link that allows you to click straight to a map? How about a link to dial a number? All possible with mobile PPC and all things that make it increasingly likely that we can drive action from these ads (see Figure 12.10).

Another advantage of PPC is speed. We can be No. 1 in the search rankings almost immediately if we are willing to pay for it. Organic search can take months to achieve rankings for competitive terms, and even then it's not guaranteed. Also, don't mistake organic search for being free. Although you don't pay for every click, you are going to spend time and effort creating content and so on.

Figure 12.10 Mobile paid search in Google

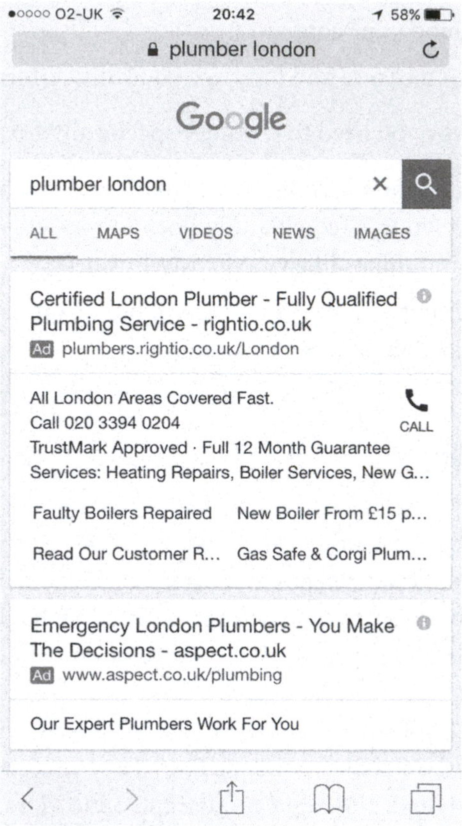

SOURCE: www.google.co.uk
Google and the Google logo are registered trademarks of Google Inc; used with permission

PPC is an auction-based system. The more you are willing to pay per click, the more visibility your ad will generally get. This also means that the more competitive your industry and the words you choose to target both are, the more expensive it can become. More on this later.

PPC fundamentals

We'll take a look at each of the key steps involved in planning and implementing a successful mobile PPC campaign shown in the list below:

- keyword research;
- create ad copy;

- select additional ad features;
- set targeting criteria;
- set budgets and bids.

PPC keyword research

There will certainly be commonality between the keyword research you do for your SEO campaigns and your PPC campaigns, and you will use many of the same tools. However, one fundamental to understand about PPC is that the more precise your selection of words, and the better matched these are to your ad copy and landing pages, the more successful your campaign will be.

The words you select for your PPC campaigns will trigger your ads. You could select a generic search term to trigger your ad so that you get lots of traffic. This is a very good way to spend lots of money and get few results. You could also use lots of different search terms to trigger the same generic ad. Again, a good way to waste your budget. Generally, a very specific key phrase that triggers a specific ad which sends the searcher to a very specific and relevant landing page will get the most from your budget.

A really important consideration when looking at mobile paid search is that of location-based search terms. A location-based search term is most likely to end in action on a mobile device (Nostran, 2016), so these terms can be highly valuable. We'll talk more about location-based targeting later.

Create ad copy

Fundamentally a PPC ad is made up of a number of lines of text (it may also include an image on platforms such as Facebook) and a link (or a number of links) through to your site. This copy is what grabs the searcher's attention and attracts the click-through to your site. We won't go into copywriting techniques here as much has been written on the topic already, but what we must think about in regard to writing our ads for mobile users is context. When I search on a mobile device, I am more likely to be at the point of conversion (actually carrying out an action) than when I search on a desktop. For this reason, the wording of my ads needs to reflect this context.

Bear in mind you can create multiple versions of your ad copy and most PPC systems will automatically rotate these ads and tell you which ad is attracting the most clicks and/or conversions on your site.

Google moves to a context focus

A very important move, that very closely reflects many of the issues we have discussed in this book, is Google moving its PPC system (AdWords) to a context-based model. What this means is that we aren't just doing one ad for mobile and one for mobile.

What we are actually doing is setting up a single campaign that has a number of different options based on the context of your search. That will include what device you are searching on, the time of day and your location. Based on this context I can use different ad options and set my bids accordingly. For a great example of this in action, let's take a look at an example from Google in the box below.

Google context-based AdWords

Sally's Flower Shop has a physical shop on Main Street and a website where customers can order online.

Within a single campaign, Sally can customize ad headlines, text and landing pages so that people using smartphones see ads that take them to her mobile site, while people using computers and tablets see relevant links on her desktop website. And when her shop is open, Sally has ads that show links to a shop locator as well as her business phone number for smartphone users. When her shop closes at 5 pm, she sets her ads to only show links to her website where customers can place their orders. With campaign scheduling and bid adjustments, Sally is able to schedule when and on which devices she would like these ad extensions to appear.

Additional ad features

Google and Baidu offer a number of additional ad options, some of them specific to mobile searches and others that are available for all ads. A mobile-specific example is a 'click-to-call' button, allowing users to call your telephone number directly from your ad. In Google, for example, you can include links to multiple pages of your website (called sitelinks). You can also add links to maps of your location to your ads.

These additional ad features serve two purposes. The first is clearly to encourage users to take an action in response to your ads. Secondly, they can make your ad more likely to be noticed as they differentiate your ad visually, and generally add to the overall size of the ad. We have mentioned several times that you are more likely to carry out some sort of immediate action after a mobile search than after a desktop search, and these additional call-to-action buttons can increase this likelihood further.

Set targeting criteria

The targeting criteria you set for your ads are particularly important for mobile ads. You can target by the type of device somebody is searching on (split between desktop, smartphone and tablet) as well as target by location-based criteria. Location-based targeting is split into three key areas in Google, and most other systems follow similar principles (although accuracy can be poor in Baidu in particular). These location-based criteria are:

- targeting by physical location that the search is made in (eg searching for 'hotels' while in New York);
- targeting by what people are searching for (eg searching for 'hotels in New York');
- targeting by intent – this is based on various factors that Google consider, such as previous searches (eg searching for 'hotels' after having searched 'trip to New York' and 'best deals flights New York').

Set budgets and bids

As well as setting your daily budget (the maximum you are willing to spend each day) you can set your maximum cost-per-click (CPC). CPC is the main factor that decides where your ad shows up on the page. Because PPC systems generally work on an auction basis, the more you are willing to pay per click, the higher up the page your ad appears and the more visibility it has. That visibility should lead to clicks, assuming your ad content is appealing to the searcher. You shouldn't always assume, however, that it's always better to be in the top positions on the page. You may find that being further down the page means you are paying less per click and getting clicks more slowly, but you get better value overall from your budget. This is one of the many reasons that, to get the maximum value from your budget, you need to test and adjust your campaigns on an ongoing basis.

CPC can be set at a number of different levels. You can apply a single maximum CPC to a group of ads or just for a particular key phrase. Many systems, including Google, have an automatic bidding option that will try and maximize the number of clicks you receive for your budget. Just

Figure 12.11 Google AdWords: adjusting bids according to device

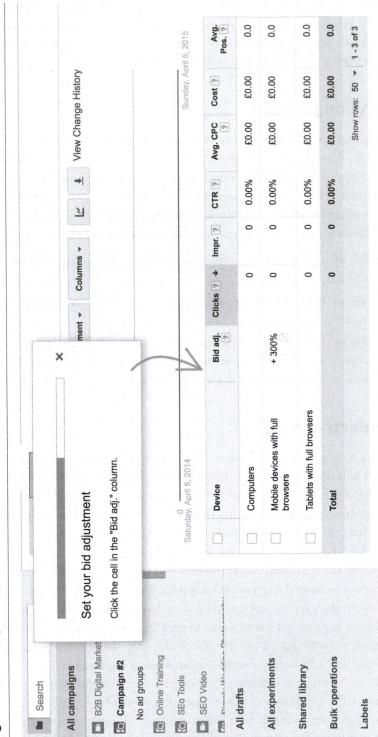

SOURCE: www.google.com/adwords
Google and the Google logo are registered trademarks of Google Inc; used with permission

remember, though, that the maximum volume of traffic doesn't necessarily mean the maximum number of conversions on your site.

Within Google and its bid adjustments functionality, you can also adjust your bids according to context-based information such as mobile devices and time of day. For example, you may decide that mobile searches are more likely to convert into business so may be willing to pay more for a mobile click. You may also find that mobile searches are less competitive than desktop searches and that you can actually decrease your bids slightly (see Figure 12.11).

This ability to target by device is incredibly underused currently, especially when you consider that in many cases a mobile search has a higher likelihood of converting than a desktop search.

Within Google AdWords you also have the option to set rules-based bidding, meaning that you do things like automatically adjust your bid (within a certain range) to always keep your ad in a certain position. This can help you automate your bidding to factor changes in competition levels.

PPC considerations

Beyond the fundamentals of PPC, there are some other things we need to consider when planning our campaigns that can have a significant impact on the value we get for our budgets.

Ongoing management and optimization

To get the most out of your PPC budgets your campaigns will need to be closely monitored, tested and adjusted on an ongoing basis. Levels of competition can change, and bids will need to change accordingly. You may find that certain keywords are working well and that others, although driving traffic, are not converting into business. Again, you will need to adjust your campaigns accordingly. This means that as well as considering the cost of your PPC budgets you need to factor in the time or cost of managing your campaigns effectively as well. We'll discuss using agencies for PPC management further in a moment.

Quality scoring

The Google AdWords system is particularly focused on rewarding campaigns that are highly targeted and give relevant results for searchers. They do this by factoring in a quality score when deciding what ads to show and how high up the page those ads should be displayed. Quality scores take into account a number of factors but look at things like the click-through rate (CTR) of your ad to signify its relevance. This means that ads seen as being relevant are given a boost in their positioning and you can actually have your ad appearing above the ad of somebody else who is actually paying more per click than you are.

Other quality factors include having the word/phrase that was searched for actually in your ad and on the landing page to which you are sending searchers. The more relevant your ad, the better your quality score and the more visibility you get for your budget. It also means that Google is rewarding relevant ads; that in turn means that searchers see PPC ads as more relevant generally; searchers should in turn click on the ads more, thus making Google more money. Clever stuff.

Conversion tracking

As with any digital marketing activity, we need to understand what impact it is having on our bottom line. We'll discuss the idea of a 'conversion' further in Chapter 19, but most PPC systems give you some ability to track beyond a click and to see what happens afterwards. After all, all the traffic in the world is useless if the visitors to our site all leave immediately upon arrival.

Working with PPC agencies

Agencies can help you get the most from your PPC budgets by planning and setting up your campaigns effectively and then managing your campaigns on an ongoing basis. They can also add additional cost and bring little benefit. If you are going to work with an agency you need to be very clear on what value they provide and if this is giving you a positive return on investment (ROI).

From my experience of working with lots of agencies, and having run a search agency, there are a couple of key things to look out for: payment terms and campaign management.

Payment terms

Far too many PPC agencies charge on a 'percentage of spend' basis. So, for example, you pay them 20 per cent of what you are spending on your PPC clicks. This approach makes no sense for a couple of reasons. First of all, more money doesn't necessarily mean more work to manage that budget. It may do, but it's really down to how that budget is being spent. Secondly, there is no incentive for an agency to save you money and reduce your budget if that is then going to reduce their fee.

Another issue to consider is campaign ownership and handover fees. What I mean by this is being very careful of contracts with PPC agencies that state that they own the campaign data and/or there is a handover fee for your campaign. This can mean you are charged to set up a campaign, but when you cease working with the agency you either have to pay them to hand over the account or start again from scratch. It can also mean that if you part company with the agency that ran your PPC, you no longer have access to the data collected during that campaign, such as which ads/key phrases were performing best, and you need to start the test-and-learn process from scratch.

Campaign management

A final consideration is how much work you are actually getting for your budget. Many PPC campaigns are managed for a monthly fee, but when the campaign is up and running successfully, it is very easy to sit back and just let things tick over without doing any work. For this reason, instead of a monthly bill that just reads 'campaign management', you need a breakdown of what work has actually been done. The Google AdWords system can actually track all changes made to a campaign over any given period, which can help you get to the bottom of what work has actually been done. Even when getting these work breakdowns, look out for the catch-all 'keyword research'. It is a valid activity, but you need to understand what keyword research was actually done and what was the output.

Mobile SEO and PPC working together

As we can see, there are some very specific considerations when looking at mobile search. We also need to consider how SEO and PPC can work together effectively within mobile marketing. My first point on this is always that PPC on mobile devices is even more important than it is on desktop devices. This is because of the much smaller screen sizes at play, and the greater amount of this space that paid search gets over organic search. It is also because many mobile searches are in relation to a commercial need, and, as we have explored, PPC results are most likely to be clicked on when the search term indicates high commercial intent.

I'm often asked whether you should bother with PPC advertising if you are already ranking No. 1 for a search term in the organic search results. The only way to truly get an answer to that question is by testing it. Look at your results with and without PPC running and you can answer the question precisely. This testing is even more necessary with mobile search, because of the different user focus and motivations. You will certainly get some cannibalization, that is people clicking on your paid ads that would have clicked on your organic search results, but you need to understand what additional traffic you can get and then look at how PPC and SEO traffic convert differently.

Mobile search: conclusions

PPC campaigns targeted at mobile users are currently underutilized, and clearly this gives us an opportunity to get more from our budgets by targeting effectively. SEO for mobile is also underutilized, due to the number of sites not being optimized for mobile devices and the search engines becoming increasingly aware of this. This means that effectively planned and implemented mobile search campaigns can be one of our most important business drivers.

Mobile advertising

13

We are going to start this chapter with some definitions and some warnings. We'll look at mobile advertising fundamentally in terms of various forms of banner advertising including video ads. The reality is that paid search is a form of mobile advertising, but we discussed this topic as part of the search section in Chapter 12. Paid social is also another form of mobile advertising and we have also explored this in Chapter 11 on social media. Another issue is that due to the number of different creative options, the term 'banner advertising' doesn't really cover all of the different things we can do with mobile ads.

Now let's move to the warnings. We have already discussed how screen space is at a premium on mobile devices; that we have slow internet connections much of the time; and that we are often very objective and action-focused when using mobile devices. All of these factors mean that any online advertising that slows down my experience or gets in my way is likely to be at best ineffective, and at worst counterproductive and damaging to a brand.

Actually, this is probably the easiest aspect of mobile marketing to waste your budget on and carry out ineffective campaigns. This is because banner ads are the easiest part of mobile marketing (and digital marketing more broadly) to understand from a traditional advertising perspective. So, many traditional marketers' approach to digital has been to create some print/TV ads and then produce some digital equivalent of these in a banner format. This approach is generally poorly targeted and not adjusted for the digital channel. Much of the blame for this lies with agencies that don't really understand digital.

The positive side of online advertising is that we now have a wide range of creative and targeting options that can improve the effectiveness of our ads along with the analytics and metrics to judge their success.

Mobile advertising objectives

Just as with any other aspect of mobile marketing we should start by clearly defining what our actual end objectives are and how mobile advertising is going to contribute to these goals. The reason this is even more important to define when considering mobile ads is because of the way they are often priced and measured.

Most online advertising is sold on a cost per mille (CPM) basis. This basically means that you pay a certain fee every time your ad is shown a thousand times, ie you are paying for display, not for clicks, and certainly not for results. This isn't the only option, but it is still the most common, and it's very easy to waste budget on views of your ad by the completely wrong audience.

Your ad being shown once is called an 'impression'. If I hit 'refresh' 10 times on a page with an ad on it, that will be 10 ad impressions. Also, if a page loads that my ad is on, but the ad is below the fold (below the part of the page that I can see without scrolling down), and the user doesn't scroll down the page, the ad will still register an impression even though nobody saw it. The impression also doesn't tell you how long the user was actually on the page that the ad was shown on. This 'page view duration' is referred to as 'dwell time', and even if my dwell time was half a second, if the ad loaded, an impression gets counted. We clearly need to look carefully at what we are paying for.

Another challenge with online advertising is that results are often measured on a click-through rate (CTR) basis. The reality, though, is that even if we get clicks it doesn't mean that the visitor that drives to my site will necessarily carry out the action that we want them to. They may leave my site as soon as they arrive. Equally, somebody that doesn't click on my ads may interact with them in some way and go on to make a purchase. We need to find better ways than CTR to measure the success of an ad.

Fortunately, many of the newer mobile ad platforms now offer different pricing models, such as cost-per-click, cost-per-install (for app installs) and cost-per-view (for video ads).

App advertising

As well as the options for advertising on mobile sites, we also need to consider ads within apps. This may be from the perspective of running ad campaigns in appropriate apps that are used by my target audience, but it may be from the perspective of making money by placing ads within our own apps.

Many ad formats are generally very similar for mobile sites and for apps and we'll look at these when we look at the creative options available to us, but there are also some exclusive options that are only suited to apps.

There is a huge range of mobile ad platforms out there, and unsurprisingly, Google owns one of the largest (AdMob). On both iOS and Android you can integrate ads from a wide variety of different ad networks (which we'll discuss later). All of these solutions generally work by automatically placing ads within your apps (in the locations you have decided in the app) and then giving you a share of the revenue made from the ads.

If you want to advertise within apps, then there are a number of different ad networks you could go to (again, more on this later) or you could approach an app owner directly to negotiate a deal.

Ad networks vs media owners

An ad network manages the advertising space on a number of different mobile properties that may include both mobile sites and apps. These ad networks may also manage advertising space on desktop sites. They offer a range of targeting options and then place your ads within the sites they manage according to your targeting criteria. Different ad networks have different targeting criteria, which can vary from fairly basic options like category matching (automotive, finance, etc) all the way through to things like behavioural targeting (which we'll explore when we look at targeting options).

Generally, ad networks charge a fee and then share some of this with the owner of the location the ads are shown in. They provide the technology for placing the ads, the account management to the advertisers and provide some form of reporting for all parties involved.

Ad networks are the reason for there being standard sizes and types of ads. This means you can create an ad once and it can be run across multiple properties (mobile sites and apps) without the need to redesign every time.

Internet Advertising Bureau

The Internet Advertising Bureau (IAB) is the trade association for online and mobile advertising. It promotes growth and best practice for advertisers, agencies and media owners. It has sites for regions around the world sharing best practice and defines the standards for sizes and types of ads. This includes the various types of mobile ads and things like how big they should be in regard to screen size, file size and so on.

The global website can be found at the following website, which also lists local market sites: http://www.iab.net.

Rather than going to an ad network, you could go directly to a media owner. A media owner in mobile marketing is somebody that owns a site or app (or even an e-mail list) that you may wish to advertise on. Going directly to a media owner has the advantage of knowing exactly where and how your ads will be shown (this often isn't true when using ad networks because much ad placement is 'blind placement', meaning you set the targeting criteria but don't get to choose the exact sites your ads show on). The disadvantage is that very often you are targeting one site or app at a time and they don't have the targeting technologies available via the ad networks. They may also be limited in the types of creative options they can offer and the reporting facilities they can give you.

Targeting options

Different ad networks offer different types of ad targeting, and I've summarized the most common ones below. A single network normally doesn't offer all of the different targeting options, and different networks will be able to place advertising on different websites. You may need to work with multiple ad networks to achieve your campaign objectives.

Location

Place your ads based on location-based criteria such as country, city and distance from a physical location. This option can often also be used to exclude as well as include an area.

Device and OS

Place ads based on device and operating system. Some networks also allow you to choose by version of operating system.

Carrier

Ad placement by network provider. This can also allow you to choose between a WiFi- and carrier-based internet connection (based on the fact you may only want to target ads when users have a fast internet connection).

Demographic

Target by criteria such as age and gender. This may be based on users having registered their details or it may be based on some sort of modelling, in which case it's worth understanding how this data is modelled and how likely the data is to be accurate.

Category

One of the simplest forms of targeting, based on category of the content within the site or app. For example, automotive, finance, etc.

Content matched

The content of the page the ad is being placed on is read, and ads are matched based on that content. This can be effective, but just because I am reading a news story about pirates doesn't mean I want to buy a boat!

Behavioural

There are lots of different approaches to behavioural targeting, but generally these rely on being able to see a user's behaviour across a website (or number of websites) and then targeting ads accordingly. I may be looking at an automotive website, but if I have just been on three websites looking at credit card deals, then it is perfectly valid to show me an ad for credit cards on the automotive website.

Re-targeting

This allows you to show ads to people who have visited your site before. So for example if I visit your site but don't buy anything, I could then be shown ads for your site on other websites.

Guide to mobile ad networks

The mobile ad network environment is massively fragmented, with new entrants with new technologies joining the market all of the time. The team over at Soom.La are doing a great job of summarizing the market and updating this information regularly: http://blog.soom.la/2016/01/top-20-mobile-ad-networks.html

---

Creative options

This is where things start to get very interesting. The number of different creative options for mobile ads is exploding. We've highlighted a few of the more common options below and pointed out some great resources for getting some creative inspiration (a black and white book doesn't really do interactive mobile advertising full justice!).

Banners

Images can be displayed with or without animation, and users can 'tap' the banner to be taken to a variety of destinations. The ad type most prone to overuse and an easy way to annoy users by taking up valuable screen space.

Native

Native ads blend in with other content and are presented in the same format as surrounding content. This is a fast-growing and promising ad type for mobile as it is less interruptive. These ads are often used for content-based marketing, presenting relevant and related content. For this reason, relevance is of the utmost importance.

> ### Facebook Audience Network
>
> Although we have discussed paid social placement and advertising elsewhere in this book, it is certainly worth mentioning the Facebook Audience Network outside the context of social media. The network allows targeted ads to be placed within a wide range of apps in three key formats: banner, interstitial and native.
>
> Initially these ads were only shown to Facebook users when they were in other apps that included the ad platform. This means that ads can be targeted based on all of the data that Facebook knows about its users, giving some very flexible targeting options. However, the ad platform can now also target non-Facebook users with more limited targeting options. If you are looking at in-app advertising or monetizing your own app, it's certainly a very good option to consider.

Expandable

Expands an ad to cover the full/part of the screen upon a tap, without removing the user from the app or mobile-browser experience.

Interstitial

Displays rich media ads either at app- or mobile-browser launch or in between content pages.

Video

Various options to place video before/after/during other video content or within other rich media formats. Video ads include 'Trueview' ads. Trueview is a YouTube ad format that gives the viewer options, the most common of which is to skip the ad after 5 seconds.

There is also an increase in the use of a type of gamification-based format, 'Rewarded video'. Generally used in games, it gives players something in exchange for watching a video for a pre-set duration of time.

Figure 13.1 IAB Mobile Rising Stars ad units

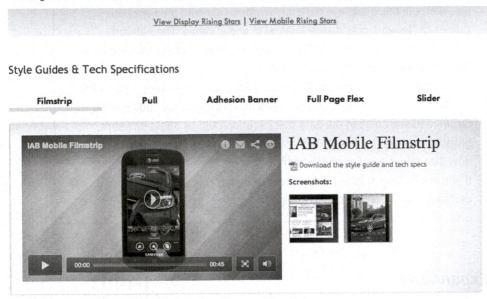

SOURCE: www.iab.net

The IAB 'Mobile Rising Stars ad units' (see Figure 13.1) highlights some of the new and highly interactive mobile ad formats, and generally gives videos to show how they work in action. These ad formats have great creative opportunities but aren't necessarily widely available and the IAB have been slow to update these.

Mobile ad features

As well as the dizzying array of targeting and creative options, there is also a growing range of ad features and functionality that can be used to encourage users to take an action after seeing/interacting with an ad. We looked at a few of these options when we looked at paid search ads, considering options like click-to-call and click-to-map. Display ads give even more options, with options like click-to-install (allowing users to install an app by clicking on an ad) and even deep-linking into a particular screen within an app.

As well as these features, which are becoming more standardized, rich media ad formats can offer a huge range of ad functionality.

Mobile ad case studies and best practice

Google's excellent Think with Google website has a huge range of examples of best practice mobile ads in practice. You can filter by topic and location and see the latest data and insights Google are publishing, all in one place: https://www.thinkwithgoogle.com/

Ad reporting and analytics

Most ad networks will provide a range of reporting tools, but ideally we should integrate our advertising data with our mobile and app analytics so we can get an integrated view of our mobile marketing efforts.

An initial step is to make sure that all of our mobile ads are tagged with an analytics tracking code. This allows us to identify any traffic coming from our mobile ads to our sites and apps and then track this through to conversion. We outline instructions of how to do this for Google Analytics in Chapter 19 of this book.

Taking things a stage further, Google now allows you to import data from other ad networks and platforms into Google Analytics so you can compare and contrast data in one place. This functionality can be found under the Traffic Sources reports and is currently titled Cost Analysis.

Google Analytics and single-customer view

Google realizes the importance of having all of our sources of data from digital marketing in one place so we can effectively analyse and manipulate the data to make smarter marketing decisions. Cost Analysis and various announcements made recently demonstrate Google's intentions to maintain Analytics as the place to get your single-customer view, allowing users to bring in and connect more third-party data sources into the Google environment.

Mobile advertising: conclusions

The mobile advertising market is currently highly fragmented with a huge range of ad targeting, features and creative options. Just like any form of banner advertising, the results of campaigns are highly variable based on the options used and the overall effectiveness of approach. For this reason, any online advertising efforts should be carefully considered and tied back to business objectives, with a clear methodology for tracking and measuring results put in place from the outset. We should also now probably realize that the term 'banner advertising' doesn't really do the more effective types of ads justice, as they actually blend into our mobile experience.

The varied, and often highly interactive, creative options available are very impressive. However, if we go back to our initial concerns about screen space, internet speed and user objectives, we need to ask some very searching questions before making assumption about the effectiveness of any mobile advertising campaigns.

Augmented reality (AR) and virtual reality (VR)

14

Augmented reality in perspective

Let's start with augmented reality (AR). According to Wikipedia, AR is 'a live, direct or indirect, view of a physical, real-world environment whose elements are *augmented* by computer-generated sensory input such as sound, video, graphics or GPS data'. And herein lies the first problem of AR: it can mean lots of different things and covers a fairly wide range of apps and functionality. We'll get the opinion of an industry thought leader later in this chapter, but let's try and simplify things a little.

In simple terms, AR overlays information on top of what we see in the real world. This can be done via the camera and screen on a mobile device, or by using some customized solution like Microsoft's HoloLens. HoloLens is the first of what are likely to be many AR standalone hardware devices. Whilst this is an extremely exciting area of technology that stands to revolutionize many aspects of our day-to-day lives, these standalone devices are not truly covered by the theme of mobile marketing as it stands (as they are currently separate, standalone technologies). However, it makes perfect sense that these type of devices will gradually be integrated with the mobile devices we use every day (although we may still need additional hardware in the form of glasses to achieve a fully immersive experience).

How augmented reality will change the world

It doesn't take a huge level of imagination to realize how radically a technology like AR is capable of changing our day-to-day lives (particularly if you watch a few of the demonstration videos on the Microsoft HoloLens website: www.microsoft.com/microsoft-hololens). Although it is early stages in the development of these kinds of products, and at the time of publishing HoloLens is still in its prototype stages, they have the potential to radically change a wide range of industries. For example, why would you ever buy a new TV or computer screen when everything you look at can be a screen? Why spend time looking at that tiny screen on your mobile device when everything you look at can be a screen? Why look at your device for a map when its overlaid onto what you are already seeing? Currently the HoloLens is a fairly large and weighty physical device, but as these devices become smaller, lighter and less obtrusive, their everyday use will become more widespread. Google had some early forays into this space with Google Glass, and although not everyone was entirely convinced, Glass was a proof of concept rather than a final definitive device. The future of mobile is definitely AR; we just don't know how far away that future lies.

There is a range of apps that offer AR, from apps that help you find your nearest pub by overlaying geographic location data onto what your phone camera sees, through to more advanced and integrated solutions like Blippar. Blippar is one of many AR apps available and it allows you to 'blipp', which basically means scanning an object with a mobile device or phone, using an app to recognize the object, and then delivering some form of defined interactive experience. For example, the screen shots in Figures 14.1 and 14.2 show a beermat that has been augmented with Blippar. This means the app will recognize the beermat, and in this case deliver an interactive experience that offers a trivia quiz and can match beers to food and snacks. This requires no Quick Response (QR) code or similar but does require the object being scanned to be set up within the Blippar environment.

Figure 14.1 The Marriot Blippar beermat

SOURCE: www.blippar.com

Figure 14.2 'Blipped' beermat launching interactive experience

SOURCE: www.blippar.com

Will search drive the future of augmented reality?

Those of you that read the first edition of this book, just about three years ago, may be slightly confused to see Blippar so heavily featured here again. Back then it was fairly early days for Blippar and it looked like adoption was growing quickly and it would become a mainstream app. Since then adoption generally slowed (although the overall user base continued to grow), and it just didn't hit the mass adoption that it needed to be adopted widely by marketers. We'll discuss adoption more in a moment, but there have been some other factors that have meant we've taken a closer look in this second edition of the book. In early 2016 Blippar received an additional US$54 million in funding, which is being used mainly to extend its engineering team and build the artificial intelligence that sits behind the platform. Blippar no longer is just a tool for marketers, but now also recognizes everyday objects. If you consider the development of search from text-based searching to the beginning of voice-based search, then 'visual search' is a very obvious next step. The 'Google Goggles' app does a very similar thing but hasn't seen much development from Google in recent years and Blippar is potentially poised to take the lead in this very interesting space. Currently, if I point my phone at a product using Blippar I may have an experience that is decided upon by the manufacturer, or one that is decided upon by the artificial intelligence behind the app. This decision-making process could be compared to the algorithm behind a search engine, so whoever can own this space will have a bright future ahead.

Adoption levels

The key challenge with apps like Blippar, that allow you to scan real-world objects and launch some form of interactive experience (without the need for a QR code or similar), is user adoption. Unless a certain percentage of mobile consumers have got the app, it's unlikely that marketers will start to use it extensively. It's also unlikely that a large percentage of mobile consumers will start using the app unless marketers are using it widely. The classic chicken-and-egg problem and one that has been faced by many technologies over the years. Time will tell what the final outcome will be, but a few things are clear.

One of the solutions to requiring the download of a specific app is the integration of AR into a current app. For example, it makes perfect sense for retailers to build AR into their existing apps to allow for the scanning of products and signage in-store to offer the customer additional information, special offers and other interactivity. The main requirement is that content offered should be valuable enough to make it worthwhile for the customer to make the additional effort to use the functionality.

AR offers the potential for huge creative opportunities and immensely useful functionality.

Beyond visual AR

Beyond the traditional view of AR, that overlays content on top of what we see visually, is a range of other AR technologies that we don't immediately think of as AR. The most common of these is audio augmentation; for example, a device that listens to the noise in any particular environment and can recognize my voice or other triggers to activate certain activities. A great example of this is the Amazon Echo, a device that combines voice recognition, audio-streaming, online service integration and smart home control. It's not the easiest device to get your head around, so it's worth taking a look at Amazon's own description (just search 'amazon echo'). This then leads us into other merging technologies of things like voice-activated agents (think Apple's Siri or Microsoft's Cortana) and then into audio search, which we'll look at further now.

With 120 million active monthly users (Pearson, 2016), Shazam is already known to many as an audio recognition platform. This basically means that Shazam can recognize segments of music and tell you the name of the song, artist and so on (assuming there isn't too much background noise and the song is in their very large database). It's incredibly good for identifying music, settling arguments about what a music track is and for cheating in the music round of pub quizzes! What's even more interesting is that Shazam has been expanded so that it can now be used to launch specific content when the audio of a TV or radio ad is recognized, meaning we can use our mobile devices to bridge the gap between TV/radio and online. In fact, they have also now expanded into recognizing print ads visually, although adoption of this aspect of the app is anecdotally currently relatively low, due to a lack of consumer awareness.

Virtual reality in perspective

Now let's move onto virtual reality (VR) (also referred to as immersive media and computer-simulated reality). According to Wikipedia, VR 'simulates a user's physical presence and environment and allows for interaction'. Again, VR is not a purely mobile technology, but as with AR, we are seeing a blurring of the lines between the technologies involved.

At its core, VR uses immersive screens that react to our movement to place us within simulated environments. VR is nothing new, and the concept has been around since the 1960s or before! (Virtual Reality Society, 2016). What has changed is that the technology required has become small enough, light enough and cheap enough to have the potential for being a mainstream consumer product.

Virtual reality and motion sickness

A common complaint of early VR products, and even with many consumer products now, is that of motion sickness (or at the very least a slight confusion of the senses!). I was lucky enough to have an early prototype of the Oculus Rift VR headset (now owned by Facebook). It was an astonishing leap forward in technology, but due to the slow refresh rate of the screens (basically how quickly and how many times they could reload the image on each of the screens per second), it confused your senses and gave you many symptoms associated with motion sickness. The longer you wore the device, the worse it got. Thankfully, many of the improvements in the technology have massively reduced these effects. However, the fact that your brain is seeing you move around whilst your body is not actually moving is a conflict that technology probably cannot easily fix. As VR grows in adoption, particularly in the world of gaming, where players are renowned for their marathon playing sessions, expect a lot more stories on the topic!

Virtual reality and mobile

At the time of writing there is a flurry of VR devices making it onto the market and the early adopters are in the world of gaming. Figure 14.3 shows the two versions of the Oculus (owned by Facebook) headsets: the PC-based device (meaning you need a high-end computer to use it) on the left is the Rift; and the device on the right, the Gear VR, is a headset into which you slot your Samsung Galaxy phone. Both Sony PlayStation and Microsoft Xbox are also launching their own devices, and this represents around 85 per cent coverage of the console market based on their current market share (Dring, 2016). However, at the time of going to press, due to limited availability of the new devices along with significantly higher costs for both PC-based and console-based devices, 87 per cent of VR headset unit sales are mobile phone-based (Raskind *et al*, 2016).

With a focus on the affordable aspect of these mobile phone-based VR devices, Google launched its 'Cardboard' device in 2014 (as shown in Figure 14.4). Although easily dismissed as more of a gimmick than a serious VR device, the platform has grown into a wide range of low-cost headsets, along with a VR app for both Android and iOS devices. A wide range of manufacturers are producing their own 'Cardboard-compatible' headsets, and many can accept a range of different-size phones.

Figure 14.3 The Oculus Rift (PC-based) and Gear VR (mobile phone-based) headsets

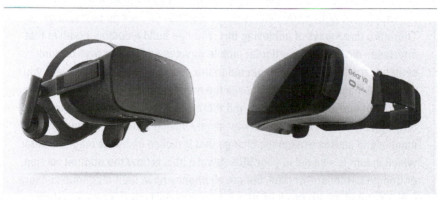

SOURCE: www.oculus.com

Figure 14.4 The Google Cardboard VR headset

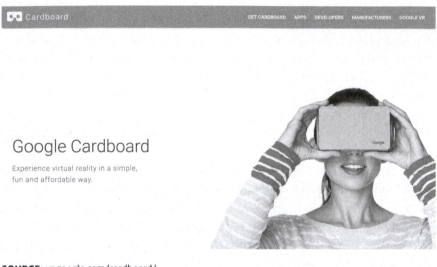

Cardboard   GET CARDBOARD   APPS   DEVELOPERS   MANUFACTURERS   GOOGLE VR

Google Cardboard

Experience virtual reality in a simple,
fun and affordable way.

SOURCE: vr.google.com/cardboard/
Google and the Google logo are registered trademarks of Google Inc; used with permission

The challenge of mobile phone-based VR

One of the biggest challenges of practical mobile phone-based VR is: how do you interact with a phone once it is placed into some sort of headset device and you can't touch it as normal? All devices currently allow you to interact with them using the range of motion sensors already built into our phones, so as we move our heads, the screen display changes (thus achieving the VR effect). But what if you want to press a button or click on something? There are three ways of achieving this. You can build a custom headset that interfaces directly with particular mobile devices and has its own buttons or switches that are directly connected to the mobile device. Alternatively, you can use a magnetic switch, that uses the magnetometer that is built into the majority of current smartphones, and therefore needs no direct connection to the phone. These devices work by simply having a switch that moves a magnet and causes a magnetic change that is picked up by the magnetometer, which in turn is a signal to your VR software (this is how the original version of Google Cardboard worked, but not all phones have their magnetic sensors in the same place, so this caused some compatibility problems). The third, and simplest, solution is to have a physical switch on the headset that simply touches the phone screen for you, making it compatible with any touch-screen phone (this is what version 2 of Google Cardboard uses).

Virtual reality and 360 images

One of the key growth factors in VR is the sudden growth in 360-degree images and how easy these have become to create and share. Both Google, via YouTube and their VR products, and Facebook, with their Facebook 360 platform, now allow you to more easily create and share 360 videos and images. They both offer platforms that can help you stitch together images and video into more immersive experiences and both have their own suggested devices for creating fully 360-degree video.

For a list of the latest resources on creating and publishing 360-degree images and video visit our online guide: https://www.targetinternet.com/360-images-a-digital-marketers-guide/.

Virtual reality innovation

For a quick insight into where mobile device-based VR is going, it's definitely worth taking a look at the Google Spotlight Stories platform (Google Spotlight, 2016). All you need to view the new VR video format is the Android YouTube app or the Spotlight Stories app for iOS devices. The platform combines a number of techniques to produce an innovative VR-type effect, where we are looking 'through' our screens into a virtual world. Not only can we move our screens around to see different elements of a story, but by focusing in a particular area of the screen, we can trigger sub-stories and change the narrative of the experience unfolding. You can also use both the Android and iOS versions along with the Google Cardboard platform for a truer VR experience. It's a brilliantly creative and clever use of the existing technologies and gives us a glimpse of how immersive the technologies can be.

Augmented and virtual reality: conclusions

Both AR and VR are still in their infancy, but their merging with mobile technologies already gives us a glimpse of how impactful and potentially disruptive they will be. It may be hard to see how these technologies will impact your organization in the short term, particularly if you work in a more risk-averse or traditional industry. However, as these new technologies are adopted into our everyday lives, they will become as second nature as search and social media, particularly as the technology gets in the way less and less.

Quick response (QR) codes   15

Quick response (QR) codes allow you to scan a square code using your mobile device, which can then trigger some behaviour within your device. Normally this means doing something like launching a website, a page for a web app or a map (we'll explore what we can do with QR codes later). Figure 15.1 is a typical QR code which, when scanned, will take you to the website that accompanies this book.

Many of us will be familiar with the concept of QR codes (don't worry if you're not, we'll get there in a moment), but the most often asked question about them is: does anybody actually use them? The answer is yes, but mostly no. Lots of people do use them but it is still a relatively small percentage of our audience in many cases. What has changed in recent years is that we no longer need a specific QR code-reading app, as apps like Shazam, WeChat and Snapchat can also recognize QR codes. My general advice is: don't use QR codes unless you have a very clear reason for doing so, and make sure the value you are offering is worth the effort of scanning the code.

Figure 15.1 QR code for *Mobile Marketing*

Barcodes have been in use for years as a way to quickly grab product details. A standard barcode can only contain numerical data on a horizontal axis. So if you want your barcode to transfer more data, you need to make it longer. This very quickly becomes very impractical.

Enter the 2D code, a system for compressing barcode data across the horizontal **and** vertical axes. These 2D barcodes have evolved to convey a lot more data in a smaller space than their earlier one-dimensional cousins, so loved by the supermarket checkout. There are a number of 2D code formats that have been developed, but the QR code format is the most widely adopted and supported of these formats.

Some of the other formats of 2D codes out there are in fact technically superior to QR codes, but it's really about adoption and how many people actually have a scanner to read the codes. We'll see this occurring as a common theme in some of the technology sections of this book. Until the adoption of software or hardware is sufficient to make the technology generally usable, we don't tend to use the technology. However, if we don't use the technology, developers, marketers and handset manufacturers tend not to adopt the technology. QR codes have got past the initial chicken-and-egg situation, but the question now is whether users really care enough to use them.

One of the major problems of QR codes is that you need to get out your device, launch an app to read QR codes and then scan the code. Although this isn't a huge effort, you really need to have a persuasive value proposition to make people do this when they are being bombarded with marketing messages competing for their attention. But, let's take a step back and look at the fundamentals of the QR code format.

QR codes in perspective

The QR code format was created back in 1994, and can handle a wide range of different types of data, such as numeric and alphabetic characters, Kanji, Kana, Hiragana, symbols, binary and control codes. Up to 7,089 characters can be encoded in one symbol. They can be read in any direction by the scanner at high speed. They also contain a level of error correction, allowing the code to be interpreted correctly if it is in any way damaged or dirty (handy if, for example, you are in a dusty warehouse or are reading the code with a poor-quality phone camera from a distance). When you create the code you can control the level of error correction, with options of between 7 and 30 per cent of the image data missing, depending on the correction level you choose. The codes are an open format and can be created by anyone without charge and the standards are internationally agreed and accepted.

You can read more about QR codes at QRcode.com, an excellent resource created by Denso Wave who created and own the format but allow its free use: http://www.qrcode.com.

QR code drawbacks

The format sounds great, but there are a couple of drawbacks. In order to store a lot of data in the code, the QR code's dimensions grow. The format is measured in modules (the small squares they are built from). It allows for codes as small as 21 × 21 modules up to 177 × 177 modules (the maximum size allows for 4,296 alphanumeric characters if you are using error correction). The error correction percentage, if increased, will reduce the amount of data you can store in the code. QR codes also have a slightly 'retro 8-bit pixelated graphics' quality about them, without using colour. You can change the colours used from black and white as long as the contrast is there for the reader to detect the pattern. We'll talk more about improving the visual aspects of your QR code in a moment.

The main drawback is usage. What a lot of the adoption reports and statistics miss is: just because you have scanned a QR code once doesn't mean you do it on a regular basis. More on that later, but what it really comes down to is offering enough value to make the effort of scanning worthwhile.

Practical applications

So we have a code system, and we can embed data in it. So what? The key benefit is shown clearly in the name: quick response. The ability to drive an immediate response or action is central to their use in mobile, and QR codes can help us bridge the gap between the real world and the online world.

Initially retailers started using barcodes to make reading product details and prices fast and efficient. Before barcodes were in wide use, retailers relied on price labels to read and input prices at the till, and there was no direct way to measure what stock had been sold. It was painfully slow, with huge margins for input error that could be costly. Inputting prices in this way would be unthinkable in today's retail environments. However, we operate in a very similar environment in the marketing world every day.

As you travel around, there is no shortage of advertisers and retailers making use of long website addresses to direct customers to their online offerings. Attempts are made to make these as memorable as possible, but have you ever bothered to actually enter these long strings of letters into a mobile phone while you are out and about? Much like the barcode, QR codes offer a quick solution whenever fast interaction is needed and can help bridge 'traditional' media and online.

QR codes certainly aren't limited to getting someone to a website and we'll explore how they are used most effectively in a moment.

QR code adoption

I'll start by saying that a global view of QR code adoption is patchy at best, and it varies pretty widely by country. In most of the world, adoption levels are very low but QR codes have been growing across China, particularly during the period 2014–16. For example, a survey by Statista found that only 6 per cent of consumers in the USA had scanned a QR code in the previous last month (Statista, 2015a), compared with 26 per cent of Chinese consumers (Statista, 2015b). You must remember, however, that just because your country shows a particular adoption percentage, it doesn't mean your target audience is going to reflect that percentage.

The most important thing to understand about QR codes

The reality is that people will use QR codes if you give them a strong enough value proposition, but should you really make them? The other key question is: is this the most appropriate way to try and drive a response?

Very often it's easier for someone to type in a simple URL or a URL that has been shortened using a URL shortener, but don't forget that case-sensitive URLs created by URL shorteners can be a real pain to type into a mobile device as well.

Latest QR code adoption figures

As with all books, by the time you read this, the data here will be slightly out of date. For this reason, you can find links to the latest QR code adoption figures and a huge range of resources on QR codes that we didn't have space to print on our website: http://www.targetinternet.com/mobilemarketing/. Or you could just scan the QR code in Figure 15.1 at the beginning of this chapter!

Making your QR code beautiful (well, less ugly anyway)

One of the main complaints about QR codes is their ugliness and what impact this has on your print materials or wherever else you are placing them. There are, however, a few things you can do about this. You can change the size of your QR code to embed a shape within it, change its colour and even apply gradients. All of these effects can be achieved for free and you can see an example in Figure 15.2 generated on the excellent http://www.qrcode-monkey.com/.

Figure 15.2 QR code with embedded image and gradient of colour

SOURCE: QR Code Monkey

Figure 15.3 QR code with image merged into the code

SOURCE: VisuaLead.com

You can take this design process a step further and implement your QR code into an image. There are a number of tools that can do this, and some graphic design companies can offer this as a bespoke service. The example in Figure 15.3 shows a QR code that links to a Facebook page, with the Facebook logo embedded into it. This code was generated using Visualead, a website that allows you to generate image-based QR codes. It's not free but the cost is very low and you get extensive reporting once your code is generated: http://www.visualead.com/.

Practical guide to using QR codes in the real world

Before you rush off in a fit of enthusiasm and start covering everything you create in QR codes, there are a few things you should always remember:

- Your customers will be accessing the resource you are linking to on a mobile device. Make sure the resource you direct them to is designed and optimized for mobile.

- Using a QR code, although quick, is still a hassle. Make sure you are adequately rewarding the customer for making the effort with something really worthwhile.

- Keep the amount of data you encode as short as possible to keep the QR simple.

Generating QR codes

If you are looking for a code generator, you can also use the Google URL shortener http://goo.gl to create shortened URLs. The nice thing about this is that you'll then receive reports on usage of your code, and as it's a Google product it's very reliable and fast. A quick tip with this is that after you've generated your shortened URL, you can look at the 'details' and see the QR code. If you then click on the code, you'll see it showing in your browser. Somewhere in the URL for the code you'll see some text that reads '150 × 150'. You can change this, for example to read '500 × 500', and get a much larger version of your code, which will be useful when using the code in print ads, which are generally printed at higher resolution than is used online.

Going beyond web links

Obviously, links to online resources for mobile users are a quick win but you can do a lot more with QR codes. It's possible to embed contact details into the codes. Want to make sure your customers can get in touch without having to input long telephone numbers and e-mail addresses? Why not embed a link to your contact details in a QR code so they can instantly e-mail or call you? Many QR code generators make this very easy to do, and the one at QRcode Monkey is excellent: http://www.qrcode-monkey.com/.

If you are embedding actual web addresses, always make sure you include the full http:// part of the address. This should ensure that most devices will recognize the type of information they are being given and launch the page automatically. If you miss it out, the user is very often just shown the link as text.

Innovative use of QR codes

This is by far my favourite use of a QR code to date, and shows how they can play a pivotal role in multi-screen environments. It's an experiment created by Google and only currently works in their Chrome browser. Essentially, you visit a website on your desktop and when the home page loads it shows a QR code. You scan this code on your mobile device and then the screen on your mobile device can be used to control the contents of the desktop site.

The QR code is just being used as a means to connect your mobile site to a custom-generated URL that then connects the browser on your mobile to the browser on your desktop. This kind of multi-screen interaction offers huge creative opportunities in the world of television and real-world events that have large display screens. Imagine going to a football match, scanning a QR code and being able to interact with what is shown on the stadium screen. A QR code certainly isn't the only mechanism by which this could be achieved, but it is a very practical method currently. Give it a try by visiting the following link on your desktop and then scanning the code with your smartphone: http://odem.chromeexperiments.com/.

QR codes: conclusions

Although we are still seeing growth in QR code adoption in the Chinese market, there is no evidence to show widespread adoption across most other markets. Now that apps like Snapchat and Shazam can scan QR codes, it may lead to an increase in usage, but in reality most users have no idea that these apps have this functionality. As visual search and augmented reality apps grow, the need for QR codes gradually declines, as these apps are able to recognize objects without any codes of any type. However, adoption levels make it hard to justify their usage in the majority of circumstances. Use sparingly if at all.

Location-based devices and beacons   16

Location-based services

A wide range of location-based services help make mobile sites and apps more useful already. Google Maps knows where I am and can give me step-by-step route guidance based on my current location. Airport Angel can tell me which airline lounges I can use nearest to my current location. Facebook knows where I am and allows me to log the location of my posts.

These location-based services are part of the real-world integration that is giving us such great functionality, and actually what we are really talking about is a range of technologies working together. Most smartphones now have both GPS and WiFi data for working out your location, and gyroscopes, magnetoscopes and accelerometers for working out the direction you're facing and the angle you're holding your phone at. This means we can create great games that take our physical feedback or apps that point us in the right direction. The bottom line is that, as most mobile devices have this functionality in common, developers will use it. If a particular functionality is limited, adoption of apps using it will be limited.

Location check-ins

Foursquare was the app that moved the idea of a location-based check-in into the mainstream. A check-in is just tagging yourself as being in a certain physical location. The app allowed you to check in to a particular location and used gamification to encourage usage. By carrying out check-ins at certain locations, in a certain order or over a number of times, you could earn badges. You could also become the 'mayor' of a location by checking in there more than anybody else. Lots of people loved this gamification. Lots more people thought it was futile and didn't see how it could be used for business purposes.

Foursquare split its functionality off into two core apps: Foursquare now focuses on local recommendations for things like restaurants and events, whilst the check-in and gamification elements have been split off into the Swarm app. Swarm allows you to share your location with friends and attempts to address some of the related privacy and safety issues, by not showing your exact location and just showing the 'neighbourhood' you are in.

Integrated data

The key challenge for an app like Foursquare is that both Facebook and Google, much bigger players than itself, are offering very similar functionality on platforms that people are already using. Why download another app when I can do everything in Facebook? Google Now, built into the main Google app on both iOS and Android devices, integrates all the data Google knows about, to try and make smart suggestions about what information you might need right now. About to travel home on the same journey you take every day? Google Now will monitor your regular behaviour and then tell you, before you leave, what the travel conditions are and how long you can expect your journey to take.

Again this raises questions about adoption levels and uniqueness of product offering. Privacy is also an issue that we need to consider at this stage as well. What are the consequences of sharing my physical location? Do I want Facebook to know that about me as well? From a marketer's point of view, all of this data is hugely valuable, but I need to make sure that I have a clear proposition (as discussed in Part One of this book) that tells the user what they are getting in exchange for the data they are sharing. I also need the consumer's trust more than ever to make sure they are willing to share data in the first place.

The opportunity of beacons

Beacons are hardware devices that can be detected by mobile devices and allow us to calculate the exact location of that device and trigger activities on the device. This type of technology is often referred to as proximity-based marketing. The most widely adopted technology for beacons is currently the Apple iBeacon standard, but this was joined in 2015 by Google's own beacon standard, Eddystone. The physical beacons are small, use very little power, so can be battery-operated for long periods of time and can be used to calculate the location of a mobile device much more precisely than with the current technology already in our mobile devices. Figure 16.1 shows an example of a beacon from manufacturer Estimote.

Beacons in context

To see the huge opportunity that beacons can offer we can simply look at the average retail journey for buying groceries and consider how it could be improved. As I walk into the store my phone recognizes the beacons in-store and it automatically launches the store's app (this automatic launching currently depends on the type of device and the beacon platform). The app then welcomes me back to the store, and because of my loyalty card it is aware of my normal buying behaviours and preferences. It can then notify me of products that I normally buy that may be on special offer and guide me to exactly where these are in-store, giving me an internal map and showing my current location. As I travel around the store I can be notified of products near me that may be of interest and the app can be integrated with augmented reality so that I can scan products to get more information. Overall my in-store experience is greatly enhanced and it connects my online to my offline experience.

Although many examples of how beacons can be used focus on retail (as we have also done here) there is a much wider range of applications. Visiting a hotel? Your phone can automatically check you in, guide you to your room and show you around the hotel facilities. Attending the hospital? Again your phone could use beacons to guide you to the correct department, register your arrival and move you between different areas with ease. The applications are endless and can be used to improve many real-world experiences in a personalized way.

One of the very few downsides of beacons, up until recently, was that you needed to have an app built to deliver beacon support, in order to be able to use them (and this is still the case with the Apple iBeacon standard). Google's Eddystone standard, however, means that we can now use beacon-enabled browsers to trigger websites when a user is nearby. What this does mean,

Figure 16.1 An Estimote beacon in a retail environment

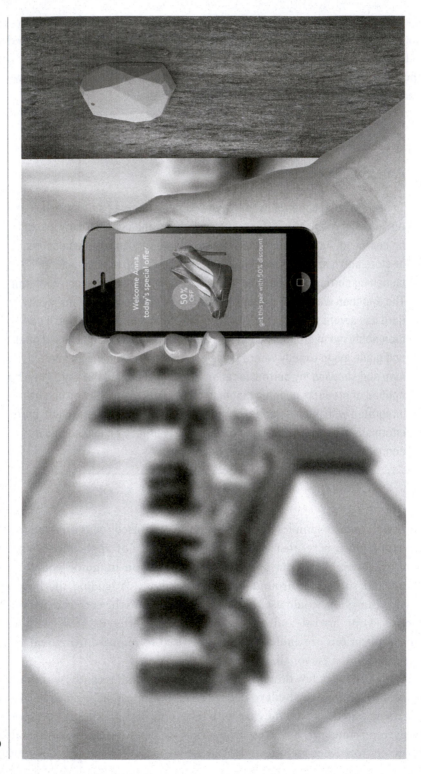

Welcome Anna, today's special offer

50% OFF

get this pair with 50% discount

SOURCE: www.estimote.com

however, is that browser-based beacon activity must be pulled by the user; we can't push notifications as we can when using apps. So when a user is in a location they may swipe their mobile device to see what is nearby, rather than app-based beacons being able to send us some form of notification. The key thing with using notifications is to provide value and not irritate our users.

Beacon adoption: conclusions

Around 84 per cent of us use our mobile devices in-store already (Beaconstac, 2016) and Business Insider expect beacon trigger retail sales to increase by over 1,000 per cent over the next 12 months (Business Insider, 2016). With the launch of Eddystone and a growing understanding of the iBeacon platform, many retailers are starting the push into beacon adoption already, and 2017 looks to be a year of huge growth for proximity-based marketing. Beacons offer a great opportunity to bring together our online and offline experience more coherently and give our customers a much more integrated and seamless experience.

Near field communication (NFC) and mobile payments

17

Near field communication

Near field communication (NFC) allows devices to interact via radio frequencies when they are brought into close proximity to one another (normally within a few centimetres). This means that I could touch my mobile device onto an NFC-enabled 'thing' and that touch can launch something, or change something, on my phone. For example, it can be used for making payments using a mobile device (much like 'touchless' credit card technology). It can also be used to launch a mobile website when I touch it onto marketing materials with an NFC chip embedded into it. The object with an NFC-embedded chip that causes my mobile device to react in some way does not require any power, so it can be put into pretty much any object.

The small size of NFC chips means they can be embedded into business cards, as shown in Figure 17.1, whilst Figure 17.2 shows one of the first NFC-enabled print ads. Each ad had an NFC chip stuck to the ad, with a message to scan with your NFC-enabled phone. The reality is that when the ad in Figure 17.2 was published, NFC adoption and usage was very low, but this was as much about innovation as it was about using NFC as a practical marketing tool.

NFC has been adopted by the majority of handset manufacturers including Apple and Samsung. In fact, NFC has been built into the majority of Android devices for many years, but Apple was somewhat late to the party, only adding NFC support in the iPhone 6. It is now, however, in all iPhones and the Apple Watch, and is the technology used to allow Apple Pay, Apple's mobile payments system, to work. Google has also adopted it as the core technology for their equivalent Android Pay system.

Figure 17.1 Business cards with embedded NFC chips (MOO)

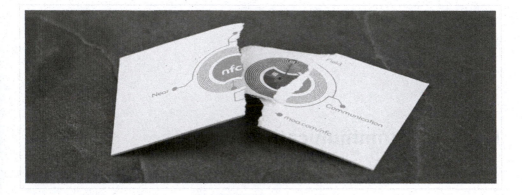

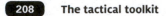

SOURCE: www.moo.com

Figure 17.2 NFC-enabled print ad in *Wired* magazine

One major difference between NFC on Apple devices and on Android devices is how the NFC can be used. Apple has currently locked down the use of NFC on its devices so it can only be used for Apple Pay. All of the functionality we've mentioned, like NFC business cards and using NFC stickers in print ads, currently only work on Android devices. This is actually very sad for the industry as it means that NFC, outside mobile payments, is not being used to its full capabilities due to lack of availability on iOS devices. This may change, as it did with TouchID, Apple's fingerprint recognition technology. TouchID was only initially available to Apple apps, but this was subsequently opened up to trusted development partners. However, at the time of writing we've already been waiting for Apple to open up NFC to developers for more than two years, so don't hold your breath!

Mobile payments

It was believed very early on that the 'killer app' for NFC would be mobile payments, with many predicting that our phones would replace credit and debit cards very quickly. Adoption has taken some time as Apple were slow to adopt NFC, but since its integration of the technology and Google launching Android Pay, there has been phenomenal growth in the usage of mobile payments. Mobile payments are expected to grow 42 per cent in the next year (Boden, 2016a) and the total value of payments made on mobile devices to have more than doubled by 2019 (Boden, 2016b).

The other key driver in mobile payments via our phones will be the developing world. Since around 38 per cent of the world is 'unbanked' – has no access to banking services (World Bank, 2015) – using phones for tracking micro-payments has huge potential and research and development is being funded by the Gates Foundation (Gates Foundation, 2016).

Instant messenger (IM) apps and short messaging service (SMS)

18

IM vs SMS in perspective

WhatsApp, Facebook Messenger and WeChat overtook SMS back in 2013 in terms of volume of messages sent (Ferguson, 2013) and WhatsApp alone was sending 50 per cent more messages than SMS by 2015 (Sparkes, 2015). However, by 2016, Facebook Messenger was by far the favourite IM, but 80 per cent of us still prefer SMS (Shmunis, 2016). The same survey also found that 48 per cent of us have more than one messaging app, hence the fall-back positioning to SMS.

> ### Blurring the lines: IM and SMS
>
> Another key factor that we need to consider is the blurring of the lines between SMS and IM on Apple devices. If you have iMessage switched on in an iOS device when you are sending an SMS, you are actually sending via iMessage, which is actually a type of IM service that can handle images and video easily (unlike SMS). For this reason, when you talk to many iOS users about SMS, they are actually talking about an IM service.
>
> Because of the limitations of SMS, and the fact that Android users are therefore 40 per cent more likely to use an IM service (Tamblyn, 2016), Google is building its own equivalent to iMessage called RCS.

Let's also consider another key factor. Over 98 per cent of SMS messages are opened, compared to e-mail marketing's 22 per cent (James, 2016). This is both the blessing and the curse of SMS messages and deserves some further consideration.

SMS is personal

The reason that SMS marketing is disliked, and the reason that 98 per cent of SMS messages are opened, both stem from the fact that SMS is about personal communications and it is interruptive. We use SMS to communicate primarily with our friends, family and colleagues, and it is far more immediate than social media and e-mail marketing because it interrupts us far more directly. An e-mail popping up in the corner of your screen is a lot more subtle than a device in your pocket making a noise and vibrating. For this reason, a poorly targeted SMS message is both inconvenient, because it demands our attention immediately, and is perceived to have intruded into our personal space.

The personal nature of SMS means that as marketers we must be highly selective in how we utilize the technology.

Types of SMS communications

In my personal opinion, you should avoid thinking of SMS marketing in a similar way to e-mail marketing, ie as a push channel that can allow you to send messages when you want to communicate with a consumer. SMS should be seen as a channel that is only used to send communications exactly when the consumer (again I use the word consumer broadly as including an individual involved in a B2B transaction) wants them.

This means that SMS is most effective if used in one of the following three scenarios:

- **Immediate response** – I request that an SMS is sent to me immediately to provide me with some form of information, whether that is a discount code or a link for an app (discussed further in a moment).
- **Planned timing** – I request an SMS at a particular time. This may be as a reminder of a particular event or contractual obligation.

- **Triggered message** – I request an SMS that is triggered by a certain event or set of circumstances. This could be when a product is shipped, when I reach a certain balance on my credit card, or when somebody tries to log into my social media account incorrectly three times.

There is another scenario, with plenty of evidence that supports its effectiveness, but which I generally will not advise any of my clients to use:

- **Newsletter and promotion messages** – a message that gives news or a special offer to an opt-in telephone number that was not specifically requested. For example, I buy a pizza on my phone via an app, and I am then sent regular messages about deals and discounts.

As I have said, there are plenty of case studies, generally from SMS marketing companies, that show the response rates and revenue generated from these campaigns, and certainly in some very limited circumstances they can be effective. However, SMS is not e-mail, and for every case study showing how well it works, there are a hundred of our friends, family members and colleagues complaining about SMS marketing messages (that is a generalization and one that I am happy to make; I look forward to debating with any SMS marketing companies that disagree!).

SMS is not e-mail. I do not want to be physically interrupted with news and special offers, unless I have specifically asked for them. Although (let's also be clear), nor do I want to be reminded at 4 am, while I am sleeping, that my credit card bill is due. My main advice is to approach SMS marketing with the greatest caution and consideration, and realize how much brand damage you can actually do if you do it carelessly.

SMS app links

A growing, and very practical, use of SMS is to send links to allow users to download apps to their smartphones. Figure 18.1 illustrates how Bank of America, for example, uses SMS to help with app download and discovery. This process generally involves having a landing page for an app within a website that is expected to be viewed and discovered on a mobile device. The idea is that a user can identify an app on the web, enter their telephone number and be sent a link to download the app directly to their phone, saving them having to try and find the app via one of the main app stores. The other advantage is that it allows the user to preselect the mobile operating system their device uses and provides data to the owner of the website about their interest in the app.

Figure 18.1 Bank of America: SMS for easy app download

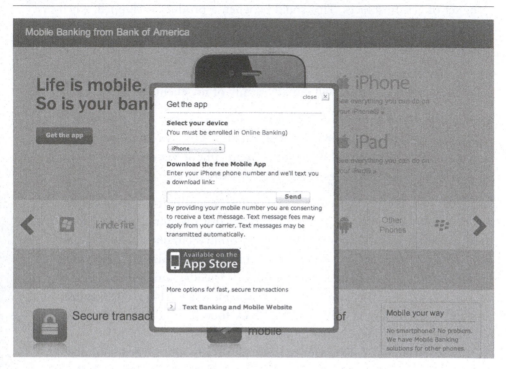

SOURCE: www.bankofamerica.com/online-banking/mobile.go

This approach is highly practical, because it fits in nicely with the user journey, saving effort when moving from desktop to a mobile app. Also, and probably most importantly, it aids app discovery. The increasing challenge is to help users find apps in the major app stores that are controlled by the app store owners (most notably Apple and Google) and have huge levels of competition for visibility. This approach means that a search engine-discoverable landing page is created that helps to funnel potential app downloaders directly to the right page in the app store on their mobile device.

IM bots and live chat

Using an IM channel like Facebook Messenger and integrating it into your website immediately offers functionality like live chat to assist customers with their purchasing decisions. However, recent announcements from

Figure 18.2 Facebook Messenger bots

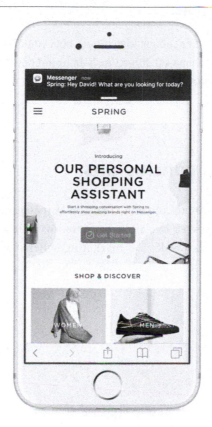

SOURCE: http://newsroom.fb.com/news/2016/04/messenger-platform-at-f8/

Facebook take this a stage further and mean you create bots, a basic form of artificial intelligence, to assist your customers with their online journey. Figure 18.2 shows a Facebook Messenger chat start at the top of the screen due to a customer clicking on a chat request. That chat can then be automated to help the customer complete their online journey successfully.

As these bots become smarter and smarter, their integration into our social media and website experiences will become more and more common. However, virtual assistants have been around for a while, and the majority of people still only use them as an amusing gimmick.

Try some live bots!

For a list of some live Facebook Messenger bots you can interact with right now, visit our online list: https://targetinternet.com/facebook-bots-and-artificial-intelligence-in-digital-marketing.

IM and SMS: conclusions

Instant messenger growth and the creation of messenger bots offers some fantastic opportunities for live and automated website and social chats.

We should only use SMS for marketing when we have a very clear indication that the target audience wants a specific message and always use SMS very cautiously.

Mobile analytics

19

In this chapter we will explore the huge opportunities that web and mobile analytics give us, and how we can move towards calculating return on investment (ROI) for our mobile marketing.

Mobile analytics means you will no longer ever have the problem of not having enough data to assess your campaigns. Your problem now will be having way too much data and not knowing what to do with it! Most organizations I look at now have web and mobile analytics (this is an improvement on where things were a couple of years ago) but the data isn't used in an effective way at all. In fact, the most use that web analytics gets in the majority of organizations is a chart being held up once a month showing web traffic going up. This doesn't say **why** traffic is going up, how it could be improved further, or if in fact it's going up more slowly than the competitors' traffic. The data is just the starting point. To be effective in using mobile marketing we need to be able to analyse that data and use it to measure and improve our efforts.

The marvels of Google Analytics

Google Analytics, the free analytics tool from Google, with over 83 per cent global share of the analytics market (W3Techs, 2016), has hundreds of built-in reports as well as a huge variety of customization options. It is constantly updated and offers a great deal of what many commercial analytics packages offer (and more in some cases!). So one of the most common questions asked is: why is it free?

Google Analytics started out life as a commercial tool called Urchin. This was then purchased by Google, repackaged and given away for free to help website owners improve their sites and drive revenue. Why does Google want you to make more money? Because then you are more likely to spend money on their advertising products, which generate 92 per cent of their income (US SEC, 2015).

There is in fact a paid version of Google Analytics (Google Analytics Premium) that gives you some of the things absent from the free version, like an account manager, telephone support and service level agreements. It also gives you even more functionality and extended access to data and customization. However, it costs US$150,000 per year (this may seem like a huge amount, but actually represents good value when you consider what you get and the fact it is aimed at enterprise-level organizations).

Google Analytics: global use and privacy

For some people and some locations, Google Analytics isn't suitable. For example, it won't work properly in China because of data being blocked leaving the country and users not being able to log in to read their reports. In other cases, people just don't like Google or want to share their data with them. If you find yourself in one of these scenarios there are a number of alternatives. There are several excellent commercial options, the market leader of which is Site Catalyst from Adobe. There are also several free alternatives, including the excellent PIWIK. The core principles of analytics remain the same and the majority of the reports we discuss here exist in these other packages as well (sometimes under different names).

Throughout this chapter we will focus on showing how you can use a tool like Google Analytics to help with every stage of your mobile marketing activity. We'll look at using the tools in practice and understand how they can be used within our mobile sites and apps.

Setting up Analytics

Most analytics packages use a technique called 'page tagging'. When you register for a Google Analytics account you are given a unique code which needs to be put on every page of your website. This code then sends information back to Google each time somebody uses one of the website pages or app screens (see the box below for more on analytics in apps). This data includes a range of mobile-specific reports.

Google Analytics for apps

You can add Google Analytics to apps and get similar reports as you do for a website. Once you have set up an Analytics account you add a new 'property' (a property is a website or an app). Once the app property is set up you are given some unique identifying code which needs to be built into your app. This is more complicated than just adding the code to every page of your website and will need to be done by an app developer.

Once the app is set up, you will get a wide range of reports that we will discuss in more detail later in this chapter. The core thing to understand is that app analytics reports generally talk about screens rather than pages as used in web analytics, but they are very closely aligned. There is also extensive reporting on 'events'. These are things that happen within a screen in your app without the need for another screen to load. You can also look at events in web analytics, but due to the nature of mobile apps, they are more widely used in this scenario.

Core reports

Once you have your analytics code in place, your analytics package will start recording visitors to your website or app. These reports are broken down into a number of different categories. I have highlighted some of the core areas of reports below. After this we will take a look in detail at some of the reports that are most relevant from a mobile marketing perspective.

Real time

As the name suggests, these reports can show you people using your website or app in real time. You can track where they came from (search engine, other websites, etc), what content they are looking at and where they are in the world, amongst other things. One of the key things to remember about real-time reports is that they can be an immensely engaging and often an utterly useless waste of your time! What I mean is that, although the data is fascinating, and it's thoroughly engaging to see who is using your website in real time, it's not easy to do anything useful with the data. It's great to see the instant reaction to an e-mail going out or to a social media campaign, but hard to take away any actionable insights.

Audience

This will tell you all about where in the world your audience is located and, very importantly, about the technology they are using to access your site or app. This will include, through the Devices report, data on the mobile devices on which they are accessing your site, the operating system of those devices, as well as the volume of mobile visitors.

Another useful report for mobile marketing is Visitors Flow report. You can use this to look visually at how people are travelling through your site (Figures 19.1 and 19.2). The great thing about this report is that it is very easy to change the way the audience is initially split up. As standard, you'll see visitors from each country and how they travel through your site, which pages they look at and where they exit. However, it is very easy to change the initial segmentation from country to mobile devices. By doing this you can explore how mobile users travel through your site and see how their behaviour differs from desktop users. This can be useful for identifying pages that may give a poor mobile experience leading to lots of site exits.

Acquisition

These reports will show you where your traffic is coming from and help you identify which of your mobile marketing efforts are helping to drive visitors to your website. You can drill down into each of the different sources of traffic and it will show you traffic from search engines, social media sites, other websites (called Referrals) and direct traffic. Theoretically, direct traffic is people that have just typed your website address into their browser or clicked on a bookmark that they have previously saved. The reality is that direct traffic just means that Google cannot identify where the traffic is from. More on this later when we look at tracking code.

Figure 19.1 Devices: volume of mobile visitors and devices used

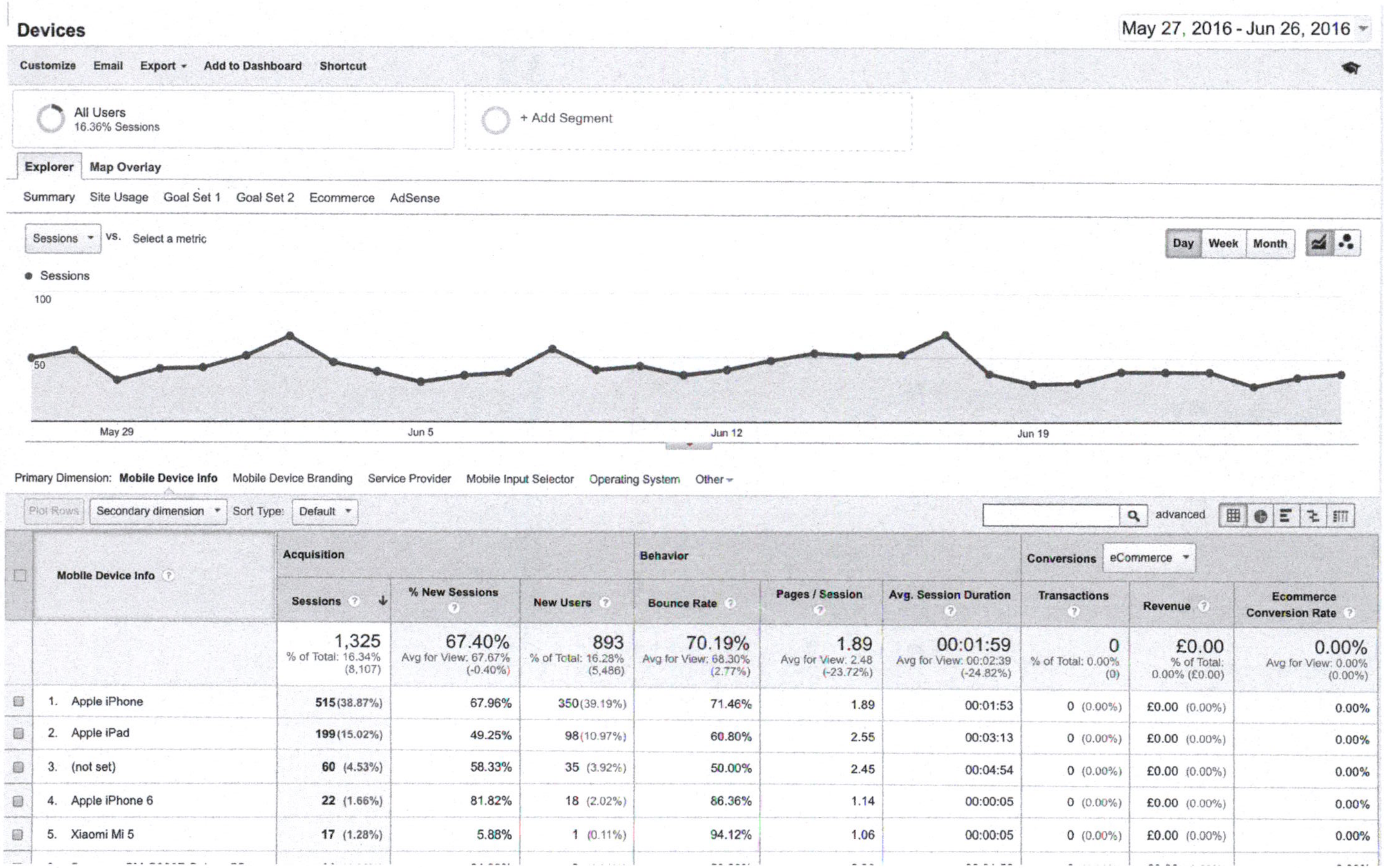

Devices

Customize　Email　Export ▾　Add to Dashboard　Shortcut

May 27, 2016 - Jun 26, 2016 ▾

All Users
16.36% Sessions

+ Add Segment

Explorer　Map Overlay

Summary　Site Usage　Goal Set 1　Goal Set 2　Ecommerce　AdSense

Sessions ▾ vs. Select a metric

● Sessions

Day　Week　Month

100

50

May 29　　Jun 5　　Jun 12　　Jun 19

Primary Dimension: **Mobile Device Info**　Mobile Device Branding　Service Provider　Mobile Input Selector　Operating System　Other ▾

Plot Rows　Secondary dimension ▾　Sort Type: Default ▾

advanced　eCommerce ▾

	Mobile Device Info	Acquisition			Behavior			Conversions eCommerce		
		Sessions ↓	% New Sessions	New Users	Bounce Rate	Pages / Session	Avg. Session Duration	Transactions	Revenue	Ecommerce Conversion Rate
		1,325 % of Total: 16.34% (8,107)	67.40% Avg for View: 67.67% (-0.40%)	893 % of Total: 16.28% (5,486)	70.19% Avg for View: 68.30% (2.77%)	1.89 Avg for View: 2.48 (-23.72%)	00:01:59 Avg for View: 00:02:39 (-24.82%)	0 % of Total: 0.00% (0)	£0.00 % of Total: 0.00% (£0.00)	0.00% Avg for View: 0.00% (0.00%)
☐ 1.	Apple iPhone	515 (38.87%)	67.96%	350 (39.19%)	71.46%	1.89	00:01:53	0 (0.00%)	£0.00 (0.00%)	0.00%
☐ 2.	Apple iPad	199 (15.02%)	49.25%	98 (10.97%)	60.80%	2.55	00:03:13	0 (0.00%)	£0.00 (0.00%)	0.00%
☐ 3.	(not set)	60 (4.53%)	58.33%	35 (3.92%)	50.00%	2.45	00:04:54	0 (0.00%)	£0.00 (0.00%)	0.00%
☐ 4.	Apple iPhone 6	22 (1.66%)	81.82%	18 (2.02%)	86.36%	1.14	00:00:05	0 (0.00%)	£0.00 (0.00%)	0.00%
☐ 5.	Xiaomi Mi 5	17 (1.28%)	5.88%	1 (0.11%)	94.12%	1.06	00:00:05	0 (0.00%)	£0.00 (0.00%)	0.00%

Figure 19.2 Visitor Flow report: how mobile users travel through your site

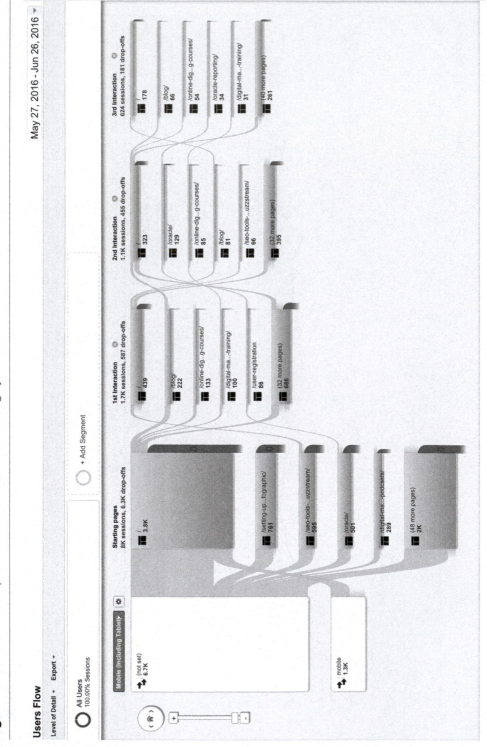

SOURCE: www.google.com/analytics
Google and the Google logo are registered trademarks of Google Inc, used with permission

Advanced Segments

Advanced Segments is an often missed but hugely powerful feature of Google Analytics that is incredibly useful in mobile marketing. It allows you to select a particular segment of your audience and then see all of the normal reports for that segment. You can also select multiple segments and compare these on the same report. There are predefined segments that you can easily select, or with a little knowledge you can build your own custom segments. Happily, 'mobile traffic' is a predefined segment, and you can therefore isolate this traffic and use the huge array of reports available to investigate your mobile audience further. You can also compare this against non-mobile visitors very easily. Figure 19.3 shows how Advanced Segments compares your mobile traffic against all other site visitors.

Another feature within the Acquisitions reports allows you to look at your Search Console data in more detail and understand the different search terms that are driving visitors to your site. By using the Devices options (see Figure 19.4) you can start to understand the different ways in which desktop and mobile users are searching.

You can also look at how different social media sites are sending visitors to your site, and again, by combining this report with use of Advanced Segments, you can see how many of these visitors were on mobile devices (see Figure 19.5).

Under Traffic Sources, you can also examine any traffic you are getting from PPC campaigns that you may be running. If you are using the Google AdWords platform you can connect your Analytics account to your PPC account and you will get full campaign reporting directly in Google Analytics.

Behaviour

These reports highlight which of your content is most popular, how long users are staying on particular pages, and look at things like bounce and exit rates. A 'bounce' is somebody entering and exiting a website on the same page; an 'exit' is just the final page in a website visit.

Figure 19.3 Advanced Segments report: mobile vs other site traffic

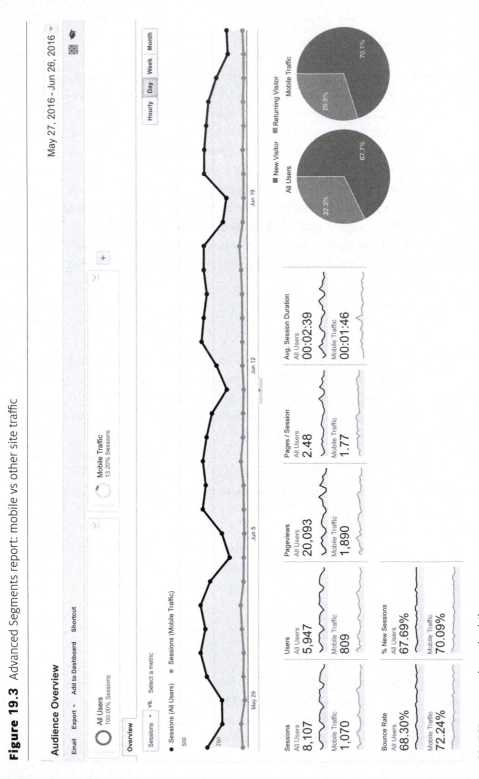

SOURCE: www.google.com/analytics
Google and the Google logo are registered trademarks of Google Inc; used with permission

Figure 19.4 Acquisition + Search Console: search term analysis

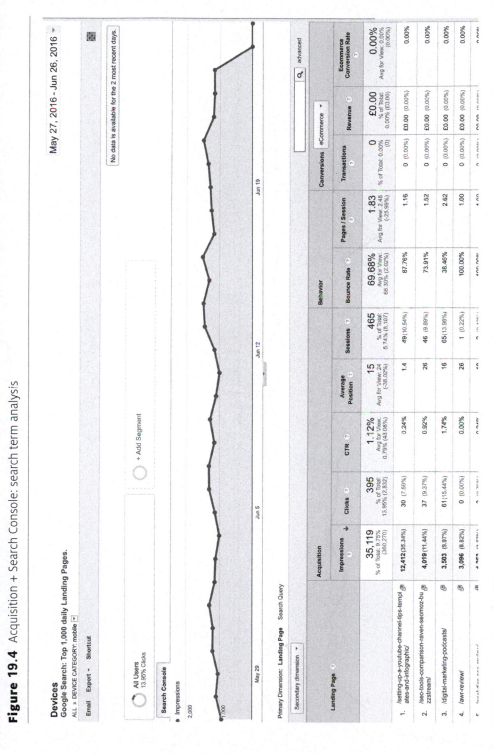

SOURCE: www.google.com/analytics
Google and the Google logo are registered trademarks of Google Inc; used with permission

Figure 19.5 Acquisition + Advanced Segments: social media traffic analysis

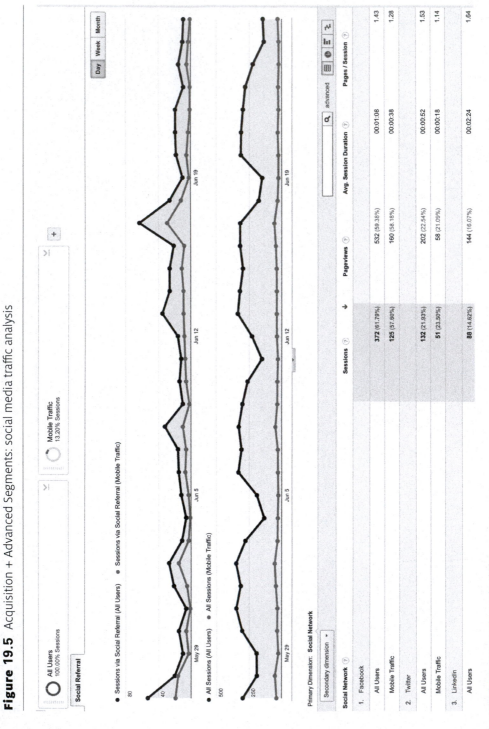

SOURCE: www.google.com/analytics
Google and the Google logo are registered trademarks of Google Inc; used with permission

> ## Not all bounces are equal
>
> We generally assume a bounce is a bad thing. For example, someone arriving at your website from a search engine, landing on your home page, not liking the look of it and then leaving, is a bounce. However, somebody bookmarking your blog because they read it every week, landing on your blog page, reading it for 25 minutes and then leaving, is also a bounce. The visitor still entered and exited your website on the same page. Therefore, a bounce isn't always a bad thing if the users have got what they wanted.

Another useful tool under the Behaviour reports is In-page Analytics. This allows you to actually see your web pages, navigate to an individual page and see the particular data for that page.

Conversions

This is the single most important set of reports within Analytics, because it is the most closely aligned with your business objectives. A conversion is somebody completing one of your online goals. As standard analytics will not have any goals set up, in order to get the most out of your Analytics package you really need to set up some goals.

A goal is a user doing something you want them to do. That could be making a purchase, filling in a lead-generation form, clicking on an ad, listening to a podcast or any number of other things that may be aligned with your end business objectives. You can set up these goals within the admin functionality of Analytics and it's worth understanding the different types of goals you can set up:

- **URL destination** – a visitor getting to a particular page. Quite often a 'thank you' page, such as thank you for buying, thank you for downloading, etc. We know if someone gets to one of these pages they have carried out an action and we can track this as a goal.

- **Visit duration** – you may decide that somebody staying on your site for a certain period of time indicates they are using your content and this can help when your goal may be awareness.

- **Pages per visit** – you may decide that somebody looking at a certain number of pages during a visit to your site is a goal for you. Always remember, though, that this could mean somebody cannot find what they are looking for and are trawling through the content of your site looking for it.

- **Event** – an event is something that happens within a page, like somebody clicking on a link to an external website, or filling in a field on a form. We can also track these things within a page. However, this requires additional code to be added to your web pages for each event you are tracking.

Once these goals are set up we will start to get Goal Reports. These show all of the goals completed and can again be used in conjunction with Advanced Segments to isolate goals completed on mobile devices. Figure 19.6 shows a Goal Report with Advanced Segments to separate goals completed on mobile devices and desktops.

Multi-Channel Funnels

One of the limitations of Goal Reports is that they take a 'last-click' approach. This means that if you look at the source of a report, it will tell you which traffic sources deliver the visitor to your site. For example, if you did a search in Google, came to my site and then filled in a form, the source of the goal would be a search. The problem becomes clear, though, if we take another example: you receive an e-mail, visit my website, then a week later you do a search and then you fill in a form. Again, the source of the conversion would be given as the search, but clearly the e-mail has also contributed.

This is where the very powerful Multi-Channel Funnels comes in. These reports tell you all of the different sources of traffic that contributed towards your goals being completed. So, for example, if lots of users are visiting via social media sites, but then visiting again via search and then completing my goals, these reports will identify this for me (see Figure 19.7). They will tell me what percentage of all of my conversions has involved each of the different traffic sources, even if it wasn't the final click before conversion. This can be hugely powerful in starting to understand the overall user journey in more detail, and how each of your different marketing activities is actually contributing towards your goals being achieved.

Figure 19.6 Goal Report + Advanced Segments: completed mobile vs desktop goals

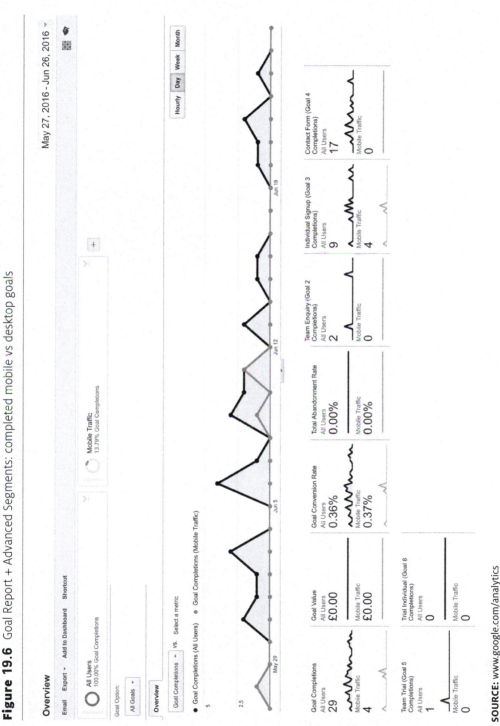

Figure 19.7 Multi-Channel Funnels: understanding the user journey

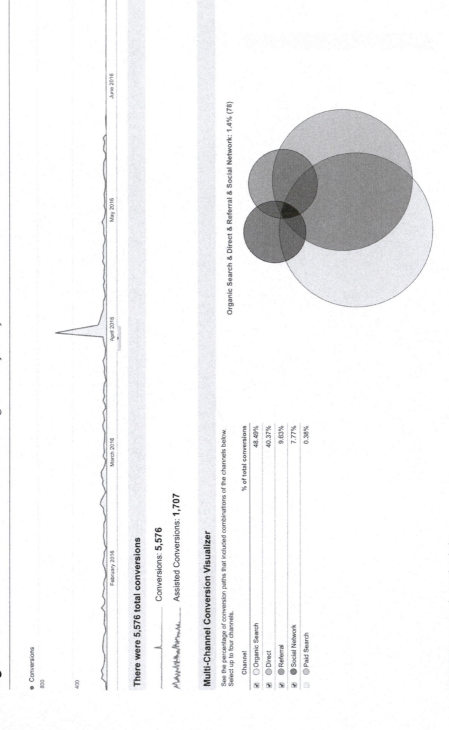

● Conversions

800

400

February 2016   March 2016   April 2016   May 2016   June 2016

There were 5,576 total conversions

Conversions: **5,576**

Assisted Conversions: **1,707**

Multi-Channel Conversion Visualizer

See the percentage of conversion paths that included combinations of the channels below.
Select up to four channels.

Channel	% of total conversions
☑ ○ Organic Search	48.49%
☑ ● Direct	40.37%
☑ ● Referral	9.63%
☑ ● Social Network	7.77%
☐ ● Paid Search	0.38%

Organic Search & Direct & Referral & Social Network: 1.4% (78)

SOURCE: www.google.com/analytics
Google and the Google logo are registered trademarks of Google Inc; used with permission

Hands-on learning resources for Analytics

Reading about Analytics is one thing, but when you come to try each of these reports out you may need a little more help. I've listed my favourite two analytics learning resources below. Both are from Google and both are free:

- Google Analytics Academy – these interactive online tutorials walk you through the core reports of analytics in a very clear way: https://analyticsacademy.withgoogle.com/
- Google Analytics YouTube channel – this is an absolute gold mine of analytics tutorials and explanations. It also includes the excellent Web Analytics TV, featuring the hugely talented Avinash Kaushik and Nick Mihailovski answering lots of user questions about Google Analytics: http://www.youtube.com/user/googleanalytics.

Tracking code

In order to track some sources of traffic through to your site you may need to use some analytics tracking code. This can be particularly useful if you are placing different versions of an ad on different devices, for example. Tracking code is added to a web link, and then when the traffic source is shown, the details you have entered will be given. Let's walk through an example to make sense of this.

If I place a link in my e-mail that drives traffic to my website without adding tracking code, the traffic from the e-mail will show up as direct traffic. The reason for this is that when a user clicks on a link in an e-mail, Google doesn't generally know where that click has come from (unless we are talking about web mail). Therefore, to really understand our e-mail visitors we need to add tracking code to all of our links so we can separate where the traffic has come from and analyse it properly.

Generating traffic code is very straightforward and thankfully Google gives us a tool to simplify things. First of all, just search 'Google URL builder'. You'll find the Google URL builder (which is just an online form for generating tracking code). You enter the page you want to link to, fill in a couple of fields and it will generate a new link for you that includes your original link and appends the tracking code. Now, if you add this to your e-mail, when somebody clicks on the link it will be reported in Google Analytics as 'Campaign Traffic' along with the name you gave it and any other details entered into the URL builder.

This can be used to generate tracking code for e-mails, online ads, links in social media sites and so on, and can help you track a particular link and the traffic it is driving to your site.

PART THREE
Mobile marketing checklists

Introduction 20

Part Three of this book is aimed at helping you implement the different elements of your mobile marketing strategy. The checklists will give you a step-by-step approach to planning and implementing the different elements of your strategy and highlight the key things you need to think about.

We started this book by talking about the importance of understanding the environment you are working in and setting clear objectives for your mobile activity. The aim of Part Three is to streamline this process and give you an easy framework to work within. The checklists highlight the key steps involved, without being too prescriptive and limiting your creative ideas. They should help you avoid missing any key issues and remember the steps that will save you lots of time and potential stress.

We start with an overall mobile strategy checklist and then provide checklists for each of the core mobile technologies and channels. The strategy checklist should be your first step. Once you feel you have ticked each of the appropriate steps off your list, you can then select the appropriate tactical checklists depending on the technologies you are using to implement your strategy.

A universal framework

Each of the checklists follows a universal framework which you can also apply to any other part of your mobile marketing, or in fact any marketing activity. This is not supposed to be a detailed strategy model, but rather a simple and easy-to-remember checklist approach that makes sure you have considered the key steps.

Benchmark

Understand the environment you are working within. This will include things like understanding your market, the target audience, the potential user journey, the broad technology options available, how your current activity fits in and any competition.

Objectives

Be clear about what you are actually trying to achieve. This step should give you clarity about the overall objectives of any mobile activity and should be aligned with a clear perspective on how these objectives can be measured. Not only will this help you judge the success of your campaigns, it will also make improving them much easier.

Tactics and technology

Select the most appropriate tactics and technology to achieve your objectives. The benchmarking and objective-setting phases of the process should help inform this stage and give you a clear view of what the most appropriate (or at least potentially useful) tactical approach will be. You also need to consider resourcing and implementation issues at this stage.

Analysis

Access, iterate and improve. Rather than being seen as a final stage, this should be regarded as a way of measuring our tactical implementation against our objectives and looking at ways to improve things. This relies on creating a clear measurement framework when we first set objectives.

For those who like acronyms, I think that BOTA (for benchmark, objectives, tactics and analysis) is simple enough to be remembered easily, and can give us some simple clarity on what is essential to our mobile marketing success. We have applied it throughout this section and hopefully you can see how it can be adopted as needed for different stages of your mobile marketing planning.

Checklists 21

Mobile marketing strategy

Benchmark

- understand the user journey and how mobile is part of this;
- assess the current level of traffic to your sites via mobile and devices used;
- assess the current site/app experience on mobile devices and identify issues and problems;
- look at the social media user experience on mobile devices;
- analyse competitor sites and apps;
- analyse search experience on mobile devices;
- assess mobile e-mail experience.

Objectives

- set clear objectives of what your primary objectives are (online sales, drive offline sales, etc);
- understand any secondary objectives such as building audience and engagement and understand how these contribute to your primary objectives;
- set measures against primary and secondary objectives.

Technology and mix

- consider how other online and offline channels will interact with mobile and map out all possible scenarios for mobile use;
- select the appropriate mobile technologies to fulfil this journey.

Analytics and measurement

- set up analytics and measurement tools for all channels;
- define how measures contribute towards primary and secondary objectives;
- identify opportunities for optimization and improvement;
- measure, analyse, improve, iterate.

Mobile site development

Benchmark

- understand the user journey and how your mobile site is part of this;
- understand user requirements and needs, and assess how the site can deliver on these;
- assess the current level of traffic to your sites via mobile and which devices are used;
- assess the current site experience on mobile devices and identify issues and problems;
- look at current site analytics and understand current user journey, popular content, drop-out points, etc;
- assess your competitor's mobile site experience.

Objectives

- define how mobile site contributes towards primary business objectives;
- set clear measurable objectives for site and tie in with measurement approach.

User journey

- understand how site is part of user journey and define content and interaction requirements;
- look at use cases, content requirements, personas and other tools to help further define user requirements and align with site content, navigation, interaction and visual design;
- optimize user experience on mobile to deliver maximum opportunity to meet user requirements.

Devices and testing

- build site in appropriate way to give optimized experience on mobile devices;
- consider the impact of building responsive websites on your content management system and other existing infrastructure;
- test on appropriate devices.

Measurement

- set up analytics on mobile sites;
- identify conversion points on site that can be defined as analytics goals;
- define tiered levels of measures (by importance) that contribute to, or are indicators of, primary objectives.

Building your app

Benchmark

- understand the user journey and how your app is part of this;
- understand which devices your target audience is using;
- understand user requirements and needs, and assess how the app can deliver on this;
- assess any competitors' mobile app experience.

Objectives

- define how your app contributes towards primary business objectives;
- set clear measurable objectives for app and tie in with measurement approach.

User journey

- understand how app is part of user journey and define content and interaction requirements;
- look at use cases, content requirements, personas and other tools to help further define user requirements and align with app content, navigation, interaction and visual design;
- optimize user experience on app to deliver maximum opportunity to meet user requirements.

Devices and testing

- define requirements for either web app or native app;
- define operating system requirements;
- test on appropriate devices.

App marketing

- complete app submission process;
- define complete app marketing plan to increase visibility and drive downloads and positive review;
- engage with audience and moderate feedback;
- improve app and resource ongoing maintenance.

Measurement

- set up analytics within apps;
- identify conversion points on site that can be defined as analytics goals;
- define tiered levels of measures (by importance) that contribute to, or are indicators of, primary objectives;
- analyse analytics, test and improve.

Social media and mobile

Benchmark

- understand how social media is part of the user journey and which platforms are being used by your target audience;
- look at existing social media experience on mobile devices and identify problems and issues;
- benchmark current social media audiences for volume, engagement level, traffic driven to sites and app downloads generated;
- assess competitors' social media platforms and content;
- identify content requirements.

Objectives

- define how social media contributes towards primary business objectives;
- set clear measurable objectives for social media and tie in with measurement approach.

Channels and user experience

- select appropriate social channels based on user journey;
- make sure all social media posting is assessed for mobile users.

Measurement

- go beyond volume and look at engagement, site traffic generation and site goal completion;
- look at overall contribution of social to site goals using 'Multi-Channel Funnels' or similar analytics tool.

Mobile search

Benchmark

- assess your current level of search optimization readiness;
- make sure search engine spiders can access your pages.

Keyword research

- use keyword research tools to identify key phrases that you need to rank for;
- identify differences between desktop and mobile search phrases.

On-page optimization

- get your identified phrases on the pages in the appropriate places:
  - page name (URL)
  - page titles
  - headings and subheadings
  - copy
  - links
  - alt text
- make sure mobile site pages have appropriate on-page optimization as well as desktop versions.

Links and social signals

- define link-building strategy focused on providing useful and engaging content;
- drive social media engagement to create social signals to boost search rankings.

Analytics and measurement

- benchmark your current rankings for identified search terms;
- benchmark your current inbound links;
- assess user journey from search terms through your sites and tie in with assessment of site goals;
- look at overall contribution of search to site goals using 'Multi-Channel Funnels' or similar analytics tool;
- adjust keywords and on-page optimization according to results.

Conclusions   22

I started this book by saying that the truth of mobile marketing lay somewhere between it being 'essential to every marketer' and 'mobile marketing is dead'. Well, now I'm going to argue that the latter point is correct and explain why that is a good thing!

You may be thinking, 'Why are you telling me mobile is dead? I've just spent hours reading your book on the topic!' It's because mobile is not a standalone topic. It is search, social media, content and everything else. What it comes down to is the user journey and understanding context.

We discussed in Chapter 12 on mobile search that Google has changed its paid search system to allow you to focus on the context of a search, rather than purely focusing on the device itself. This approach frames why we need to think about mobile marketing more broadly. It's not about the device; it's about the user journey and the context of that journey.

As the variety of mobile devices increases and the environment we work in becomes more complex, we need to focus on something other than the technology when planning our mobile marketing. Understanding the user journey is key to this, as it allows us to focus on context rather than technology.

Many organizations claim to be focused on the needs of their target audience. Most aren't. The increasing impact of mobile means that organizations that don't truly understand their audiences and the multi-device journey they are taking online will fail.

Focus on core business objectives and marketing principles, apply the appropriate technology by understanding the user journey, and then measure and improve against your defined objectives. That's it.

I wish you the very best of luck with your mobile marketing efforts and really encourage you to get in contact.

Twitter: @danielrowles

E-mail: danielrowles@me.com

Latest reports, trends and case studies

Don't forget that we have compiled a huge range of resources on mobile marketing on our site and this is updated regularly. You can also download our digital marketing podcasts. The site is of course responsively designed for your mobile devices and we have a web app you can add to your device: http://www.targetinternet.com/mobilemarketing.

REFERENCES

Chapter 2: Understanding the user journey

Criteo (2016) Travel Flash Report [online] http://www.criteo.com/media/4290/travel-report-q2-2016-pdf.pdf [last accessed 8 July 2016]

Gevelber, L (2016) How dayparting can help you tap into consumer micro-moments, Think with Google. Available from: https://www.thinkwithgoogle.com/articles/dayparting-consumer-micro-moments.html [last accessed 8 July 2016]

Kaushik, A (2016) Occam's Razor [blog]. Available from: http://www.kaushik.net/avinash/ [last accessed 8 July 2016]

McMahon, J (2016) Ford turns the driverless car into a driving movie theatre, *Forbes*. Available from: http://www.forbes.com/sites/jeffmcmahon/2016/03/07/ford-turns-driverless-cars-into-mobile-movie-theaters/#6a5b312554d7 [last accessed 8 July 2016]

TheJTHolmes (2011) Xtreme Booking 1 – Hotel Booked in Freefall [online video]. Available from: http://www.youtube.com/watch?v=Q7eHinI95rc [last accessed 8 July 2016]

Think with Google (2016) Understanding how micro-moments influence consumers, *Think with Google*. Available from: https://www.thinkwithgoogle.com/topics/mobile.html [last accessed 8 July 2016]

Young, H (2016) SalesForce blog: New research reveal how people will spend time multi-screening during Super Bowl 50, 4 February. Available from: https://www.salesforce.com/blog/2016/02/super-bowl-research-second-screen.html [last accessed 8 July 2016]

Chapter 3: Technology change and adoption

China Daily (2016) China Telecom to boost 4G user penetration rate to 80%, 20 January. Available from: http://www.chinadaily.com.cn/business/2016-01/20/content_23158262.htm [last accessed 8 July 2016]

GSM Association (2016) *The Mobile Economy 2016* [online] https://www.gsmaintelligence.com/research/?file=97928efe09cdba2864cdcf1ad1a2f58c&download [last accessed 8 July 2016]

Index Mundi (nd) [online] http://www.indexmundi.com/world/age_structure.html [last accessed 7 September 2016]

Jones, C (2013) China carriers smartphone 3G penetration only at 22%, *Forbes*, 24 February. Available from: http://www.forbes.com/sites/chuckjones/2013/02/24/china-carriers-smartphone-3g-penetration-only-at-22/ [last accessed 8 July 2016]

Chapter 4: Disruption and integration

The Telegraph (2011) Britons spend more time driving than socialising. *The Telegraph*, 28 January. Available from: http://www.telegraph.co.uk/motoring/news/8287098/Britons-spend-more-time-driving-than-socialising.html and see too http://www.gov.uk/government/uploads/system/uploads/attachment_data/file/457752/nts2014-01.pdf [last accessed 7 September 2016]

UPS (2016) Pulse of the Online Shopper. Available at: https://solvers.ups.com/assets/2016_UPS_Pulse_of_the_Online_Shopper.pdf [last accessed 8 July 2016]

Williams, TA (2016) Paying for digital news: The rapid adoption and current landscape of digital subscriptions at US newspapers, *American Press Institute*, 29 February. Available from: https://www.americanpressinstitute.org/publications/reports/digital-subscriptions/single-page/

Chapter 5: Devices, platforms and technology

Work, S (2011) How loading time affects your bottom line, *Kissmetrics* [blog]. Available from: http://blog.kissmetrics.com/loading-time/ [last accessed 8 July 2016]

Chapter 6: The future of mobile marketing

Fallon, S (2009) The Mindflex Brainwave game gives me a headache. *Gizmodo*, 11 April. Available from: http://gizmodo.com/5396971/the-mindflex-brainwave-game-gives-me-a-headache [last accessed 8 July 2016]

Chapter 8: Mobile sites and responsive design

Sterling, G (2016) Mobile devices now driving 56 per cent of traffic to top sites, *Marketing Land*. Available from: http://marketingland.com/mobile-top-sites-165725 [last accessed 8 July 2016]

Monetate (2016) Mobile-optimized sites conversion rates, *Monetate*. Available from: http://www.monetate.com/resources/research/

W3Techs (nd) Usage statistics and market share of WordPress for websites, *W3Techs*. Available from: https://w3techs.com/technologies/details/cm-wordpress/all/all [last accessed 7 September 2016]

Chapter 9: Mobile and e-mail

Lewkowicz, K (2016) April email market share: Mobile rises to 56%, its highest point yet, *Litmus*, 10 May. Available from: https://litmus.com/blog/mobile-rises-to-56-market-share-longest-sustained-growth-in-2016 [last accessed 8 July 2016]

MailChimp (2016) Effects of list segmentation on email marketing stats [online] http://mailchimp.com/resources/research/effects-of-list-segmentation-on-email-marketing-stats/ [last accessed 8 July 2016]

Chapter 10: How to build an app

Gartner (2015) [online] http://www.gartner.com/newsroom/id/3143718 [last accessed 7 September 2016]

NetMarketShare (2016) Mobile/tablet operating system market share [online] https://www.netmarketshare.com/operating-system-market-share.aspx?qprid=8&qpcustomd=1

Nike (2016) Nike Training Club. Available from: http://www.nike.com/us/en_us/c/womens-training/apps/nike-training-club [last accessed 8 July 2016]

Perez, S (2016) Apple's App Store hits 2M apps, 130MB downloads, $50B paid to developers, *Techcrunch*, 13 June. Available from: https://techcrunch.com/2016/06/13/apples-app-store-hits-2m-apps-130b-downloads-50b-paid-to-developers/

Quixey (2015) *Quixey Consumer Mobile Survey*, 22 December. Available from: https://www.quixey.com/blog/quixey-survey-reveals-the-mobile-experience-is-broken-consumers-want-all-the-value-of-apps-but-in-an-easier-more-conveni-ent-way [last accessed 8 July 2016]

Chapter 11: Social media and mobile

Khalaf, S (2015) Seven years into the mobile revolution: Content is king... again, 26 August. Available from: http://flurrymobile.tumblr.com/post/127638842745/seven-years-into-the-mobile-revolution-content-is [last accessed 8 July 2016]

Lee, K (2014) The social media frequency guide: How often to post to Facebook, Twitter, LinkedIn, and more, *FastCompany*, 15 April. Available from: http://www.fastcompany.com/3029019/work-smart/the-social-media-frequency-guide-how-often-to-post-to-facebook-twitter-linkedin-a [last accessed 8 July 2016]

Sterling, G (2016) Nearly 80 per cent of social media time now spent on mobile devices, *Marketing Land*, 4 April. Available from: http://marketingland.com/facebook-usage-accounts-1-5-minutes-spent-mobile-171561 [last accessed 8 July 2016]

W3Techs (nd) Usage statistics and market share of WordPress for websites, *W3Techs*. Available from: https://w3techs.com/technologies/details/ta-googleanalytics/all/all [last accessed 8 July 2016]

Yeung, K (2016) Twitter starts growing again (slowly): 5 million new active users in Q1 2016, *VentureBeat*, 26 April. Available from: http://venturebeat.com/2016/04/26/twitter-starts-growing-again-5-million-new-active-users-in-q1-2016/ [last accessed 8 July 2016]

YouGov (2016) Concerns over privacy [online] https://d25d2506sfb94s.cloudfront.net/cumulus_uploads/document/lcergepzz1/tabs_HP_Facebook_20160425.pdf [last accessed 8 July 2016]

Chapter 12: Mobile search

Dinan, Bill (2010) Google click-to-call: keeping it simple, *Search Engine Land*, 20 April. Available from: http://searchengineland.com/google-click-to-call-keeping-it-simple-40324

Google (2016) Google Crawlers [online] https://support.google.com/webmasters/answer/1061943?hl=en [last accessed 8 July 2016]

Meola, A (2016) Mobile search and YouTube continue to drive Google ad revenue, *Business Insider,* 22 April. Available from: http://www.businessinsider.com/mobile-search-and-youtube-continue-to-drive-google-ad-revenue-2016-4?IR=T [last accessed 8 July 2016]

Nostran, VJ (2016) 70% of mobile searches lead to online action within an hour, *MissionFound*, 17 January. Available from: http://missionfound.com/70-of-mobile-searches-lead-to-online-action-within-an-hour/ [last accessed 7 September 2016]

Chapter 13: Mobile advertising

IAB (2014) IAB homepage. Available from: http://www.iab.net [last accessed 8 July 2016]

IAB (2014) Mobile Rising Stars Ad Units. IAB 4 Jul. Available from: http://www.iab.net/risingstarsmobile [last accessed 8 July 2016]

Chapter 14: Augmented reality (AR) and virtual reality (VR)

Amazon (2016) Amazon Echo (Product) Available at: https://www.amazon.com/ Amazon-Echo-Bluetooth-Speaker-with-WiFi-Alexa/dp/B00X4WHP5E [last accessed 8 July 2016]

Blippar (2016) Blippar homepage. Available from: http://www.blippar.com/ [last accessed 8 July 2016]

Dring, C (2016) How did the UK games market perform in 2015? MCVUK, 14 January. Available from: http://www.mcvuk.com/news/read/the-year-that-was-2015-in-numbers/0161201 [last accessed 8 July 2016]

Facebook 360 (2016) Available from: https://facebook360.fb.com/ [last accessed 8 July 2016]

Google Cardboard (2016) Available from: https://vr.google.com/cardboard/ [last accessed 8 July 2016]

Google Play (2016) Google Goggles app. Available from: https://play.google.com/ store/apps/details?id=com.google.android.apps.unveil&hl=en_GB [last accessed 8 July 2016]

Google Spotlight (2016) https://atap.google.com/spotlight-stories [last accessed 7 September 2016]

HoloLens (2016) HoloLens homepage. Available from: https://www.microsoft.com/ microsoft-hololens/en-us [last accessed 8 July 2016]

Pearson, AJ (2015) Shazam news homepage. Available from: http://news.shazam. com/news/name-that-tune-millions-of-music-lovers-flock-to-shazam-175931 [last accessed 7 September 2016]

Raskind, C, Waltzer, S, Watkins, D, Mawston, N, Upadhyay, OW and Nair, R (2016) *Strategy Analytics*, Strategy Analytics press releases. Available from: https://www. strategyanalytics.com/strategy-analytics/news/strategy-analytics-press-releases/ strategy-analytics-press-release/2016/04/13/strategy-analytics-oculus-rift-htc-vive-sony-playstation-vr-will-dominate-$895-million-virtual-reality-headset-market-in-2016-on-just-13-of-unit-shipments#.V3A0YOYrK35 [last accessed 8 July 2016]

Virtual Reality Society (2016) History of virtual reality. Available from: http:// www.vrs.org.uk/virtual-reality/history.html [last accessed 8 July 2016]

Chapter 15: Quick response (QR) codes

Statista (2015a) Online activities: Number of internet users who scanned a QR code within the last month in the United States (USA) from autumn 2013 to spring 2015 (in millions) [online] http://www.statista.com/statistics/368859/ internet-users-who-scanned-a-qr-code-within-the-last-month-usa/ [last accessed 8 July 2016]

Statista (2015b) Which of these activities did you do while out shopping for your last purchase? [online] http://www.statista.com/statistics/375031/smartphone-activities-during-shopping-china/ [last accessed 8 July 2016]

Chapter 16: Location-based devices and beacons

Beaconstac (2016) In-store mobile usage. Available from: https://www.beaconstac.com/pdf/How_brands_and_retailers_can_go_Omni_Channel_using_Beacons_Ebook.pdf [last accessed 8 July 2016]
Business Insider (2016) [online] http://uk.businessinsider.com/beacons-impact-billions-in-retail-sales-2015-2 [last accessed 7 September 2016]

Chapter 17: Near field communication (NFC) and mobile payments

Boden, R (2016a) Mobile payments to grow 42% in 2016, NFCworld, 20 June. Available from: http://www.nfcworld.com/2016/06/20/345670/mobile-payments-grow-42-2016/ [last accessed 8 July 2016]
Boden, R (2016b) Global mobile payment market to hit $620bn in 2016, NFCworld, 4 February. Available from: http://www.nfcworld.com/2016/02/04/341939/global-mobile-payment-revenue-to-hit-620bn-in-2016/ [last accessed 8 July 2016]
Gates Foundation (2016) What we do: Financial services for the poor. Available from: http://www.gatesfoundation.org/What-We-Do/Global-Development/Financial-Services-for-the-Poor [last accessed 8 July 2016]
World Bank (2015) Massive drop in number of unbanked, says new report. *The World Bank*, 15 April. Available from: http://www.worldbank.org/en/news/press-release/2015/04/15/massive-drop-in-number-of-unbanked-says-new-report [last accessed 8 July 2016]

Chapter 18: Instant messenger (IM) apps and short messaging service (SMS)

Ferguson, T (2013) Chat app messages overtake SMS, *Mobile World Live*, 29 April. Available from: http://www.mobileworldlive.com/featured-content/top-three/chat-app-messages-overtake-sms-report/ [last accessed 2 September 2016]

James, K (2016) SMS: Communication through text messaging, *Textedly*, 8 June. Available from: https://www.textedly.com/blog/sms-marketing-9 [last accessed 7 September 2016]

Shmunis, C (2015) Infographic: RingCentral survey shows just how much texting matters at work, *RingCentral*, 21 May. Available from: https://blog.ringcentral.com/2015/05/ringcentral-survey-shows-just-how-much-texting-matters-at-work/?doing_wp_cron=1432780847.4377450942993164062500 [last accessed 7 September 2016]

Sparkes, M (2015) WhatsApp overtakes text messages, *The Telegraph*, 12 January. Available from: http://www.telegraph.co.uk/technology/news/11340321/WhatsApp-overtakes-text-messages.html [last accessed 7 September 2016]

Tamblyn, T (2016) Google plans to replace SMS with a new type of instant message called RCS, *Huffington Post*, 23 February. Available from: http://www.huffingtonpost.co.uk/2016/02/23/google-plans-to-replace-sms-with-a-new-type-of-instant-message-called-rcs_n_9297140.html [last accessed 7 September 2016]

Chapter 19: Mobile analytics

US SEC (Securities and Exchange Commission) (2015) Google Revenue [online] https://abc.xyz/investor/pdf/20151231_alphabet_10K.pdf [last accessed 8 July 2016]

W3Techs (2016) Usage statistics and market share of Google Analytics for websites, *W3Techs*. Available from: https://w3techs.com/technologies/details/ta-googleanalytics/all/all [last accessed 8 July 2016]

INDEX

Note: Page numbers in *italics* indicate Figures or Tables.